C000136688

Shakespeare's Dark Secrets - Revealed

Property of:
Nigel Marlow,
18, Rivett's Meadow Close,
Thorpe Astley, Leicester
LE3 3TB. Tel: 0116 299 2535

Shakespeare's Dark Secrets - Revelaed
Copyright © Arthur Marlowe 2006

All rights reserved.

No part of this book may be reproduced in any form by
photocopying or any electronic or mechanical means,
including information storage or retrieval systems,
without permission in writing from both the copyright
owner and the publisher of the book.

ISBN 978-184426-507-7

First Published December 2003 by UPSO Ltd

This edition published 2008 by
UPFRONT PUBLISHING LTD
Peterborough, England.

*Dedicated to Babs Faulkner for understanding,
Robert Hemingway for assistance, Dr Levi Fox OBE
for encouragement and all the individuals and
organisations who have helped me over the years.*

Shakespeare's Dark Secrets - Revealed

An archaeological investigation
Into the poet's private life

by

Arthur Marlowe

Edited by Brian Paine

THE LIAISONS OF MARY FITTON

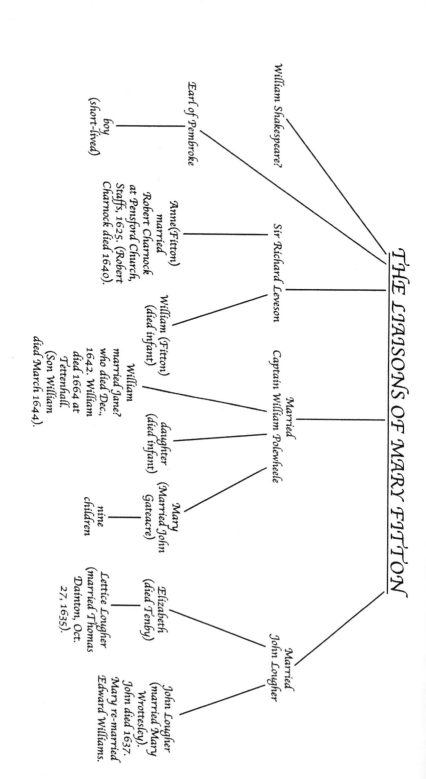

William Shakespeare?

Earl of Pembroke
— boy (short-lived)

Sir Richard Leveson

Married
Captain William Polewheele

Married
John Lougher

Anne(Fitton)
married
Robert Charnock
at Pensford Church,
Staffs, 1625. (Robert
Charnock died 1640).

William (Fitton)
(died infant)

William
married Jane?
who died Dec.,
1642. William
died 1664 at
Tettenhall.
(Son William
died March 1644).

daughter
(died infant)

Mary
(Married John
Gateacre)
— nine children

Elizabeth
(died Tenby)

Lettice Lougher
(married Thomas
Dainton, Oct.
27, 1635).

John Lougher
(married Mary
Wrottesley).
John died 1637.
Mary re-married
Edward Williams.

EDITOR'S INTRODUCTION

The facts about William Shakespeare could be written on the back of a postcard. That said, the quest for fresh information, the thirst for knowledge about the most illustrious and enigmatic figure of English literature, goes on unabated.

Amateur archaeologist Arthur Marlowe joined this search in the late 1950s, but with a different aim - to "find" the man. He wanted to know what made him tick. He was more interested in Shakespeare the person than the writer. What made him what he was? Who inspired the emotional prose? What was he really like?

Modern technology became Arthur's constant companion. Initially, he financed the research from his own pocket. But it soon became obvious that his resources would not be sufficient to support his efforts to literally dig for the truth. He needed assistance

Arthur Marlowe
...digging for the truth about Shakespeare and his contemporaries

on a massive scale to arrange complex archaeological explorations - and he received it from the Army, RAF, various ministries, university departments and private companies who put state-of-the-art scientific equipment at his disposal.

Without their valuable help, his venture into the private life of the bard would have ended soon after the first probe of the endoscope. The use of such hi-tech equipment has unveiled evidence left by the poet's contemporaries and has also confirmed some of the theories about the Dark Lady debate.

Scholars have long recognised the importance of this compelling woman in the emotional make-up of William Shakespeare, yet a lack of information about her has been a hindrance. There are plenty of candidates for the role, each supposedly offering a solution to the mystery of who she was, and a major part of Arthur's research has been devoted to trying to find the answer.

It is time the veneer which has surrounded Shakespeare for so long was stripped away. This book is aimed at the man and woman in the street just as much as the curious acadamic. It is not exactly Shakespeare in the raw, but it is a warts-and-all view of the man. Some parts may be regarded as racy, others decidedly low key. The digs, the painstaking, finger-numbing hours spent drilling through church floors - often for no result - are, in many ways, the backbone of the whole work. Without the dedication of Arthur and his team of helpers, none of the challenging opinions about the dramatist's life could have been reached. Robert Hemingway, a former

Arthur Marlowe
(author)

journalist colleague, now deceased, also played a prominent part in collating facts and figures during the digs.

Arthur is worth a story himself. He came to his hobby in an unusual fashion. I first met him in the Leicestershire town of Market Harborough where I was the editor of the local newspaper. He was a traffic warden and more likely to quote you a passage from the sonnets than give you a ticket for parking injudiciously. People actually liked this traffic warden!

The reason he was walking the streets had nothing to do with a love of officialdom. It was fresh air he sought - the outdoor life, free of the pressures which had brought on illness at Loughborough University.

A former geology engineer, he worked as an assistant in the radiography department at Loughborough after a stint as a lab technician at Leicester University. This was in the mid-60s. His interest in Shakespeare began to develop and he was awarded a grant to actively pursue his investigations. But ill health meant he had to leave university and he became a park attendant in Leicester before, eventually, donning the feared black and yellow cap.

Now retired and in his early eighties, he is still searching for the truth about Shakespeare. He is a member of the Institute of Science and Technology at Imperial College, London and his papers about the bard have been accepted by the Shakespeare Birthplace Trust in Stratford and the Folger Library in Washington, America.

Long may he continue to ruffle the stuffed shirts of the Establishment.

Brian Paine
editor

Contents

Part 1

Part 2

PART I

CHAPTER 1

An age of romance

"For I have sworn thee fair, and thought thee bright,
Who are as black as hell, as dark as night."

Ever since William Shakespeare wrote his venemous sonnet 147, the hunt has been on to identify the woman "as black as hell, as dark as night" who was at the heart of a love affair which blossomed and faded more than 400 years ago.

Many have tried and failed, following false trails and stumbling through a maze of misinformation. The Dark Lady remained a wraith-like creature with a veil drawn across her features. Why, then, should anyone spend over 40 years trying to establish the identity of this elusive seductress of the sonnets?

Well, perhaps modern technology can help solve the mystery which has defied conventional investigation. I turned to ground radar scanners, proton magnetometers, endoscopes and aerial photography to assist my archaeological exploration. It has meant digging up facts - and bodies - along a route littered with pitfalls.

But now I believe I know the Dark Lady's identity. And, what is more, I know where she is. The problem is that proving it means opening a tomb that church authorities seem determined to keep sealed, even though the coffins in the tomb could contain the most momentous artefact of English history - an unknown, original Shakespeare sonnet.

I have tried to gain permission to open this tomb, but

William Shakespeare
... familiar woodcut of the bard

without success. In the interests of archaeology, as well as literary knowledge, I believe it should be opened, so that this mystery can be cleared up once and for all.

Often, over the years, I discovered I was the first person in centuries to set eyes on wills and testaments which had laid undisturbed in archives. I also learned that evidence had been destroyed. The Dark Lady was at the heart of my research, but, of course, the other subject of Shakespeare's affection in the sonnets, the Fair Youth, played a prominent role. Who was he and what contribution did his relationship make to the poet's passionate prose?

Opening long forgotten vaults, I saw nameplates had been removed from coffins and attempts made to burn skeletons with lime. The contents of archives had been burned in the Civil War and the documents which went up in smoke referred to a specific period concerning the history of the woman I believe was the Dark Lady and her family. The material before and after this period was untouched.

It is true that, sometimes, while reading letters from the past, you feel you are prying into private correspondence, but this must be done to extract the truth and despite the obstacles and disappointments, I have found sufficient evidence to convince myself that the Victorians encouraged a myth to develop about Shakespeare...that because he wrote such elegant prose, he could not have been remotely interested in the basic desires of the flesh.

I don't accept this at all. It should be remembered that he

was living and working in the most exhilarating period of English history, surrounded by glittering personalities and by all the temptations that success could bring. The contention that this brilliant playwright and poet was also a red-blooded Renaissance man as emotional as other eminent Elizabethans may hardly raise an eyebrow in these permissive times. To the Victorians, the thought that he indulged in a tempestuous romance with a lady of the court was disturbing enough, but the very suggestion that one with so lofty a reputation may have had bi-sexual tendencies was too much for them to stomach.

My contention is that they were determined to cover up the whole saga.

The fact that he was married while everything was going on served only to strengthen their resolve to remove the evidence. They would try to forget, even if they could not forgive.

Someone once said that behind every successful man there is a woman. This is exactly where my research is aimed: find the lady (in this case, the Dark Lady) and you may find out about the man. And, at the same time, through her contemporaries, discover what Shakespeare was like as a person. The friends of Shakespeare are so real to me after all these years that, whenever a particular enquiry may help my case, I say to my team of helpers: "Let's dig down and have a chat with whoever's there." You can learn an enormous amount by examining old remains. The "shades" of Shakespeare's colleagues still have plenty to say.

A great deal of my work might not have been necessary if the Victorians had not adopted such a prudish attitude. They wrote articles and books arguing that Shakespeare imagined a love triangle...that no Dark Lady or Fair Youth really existed. They wanted to maintain the clean-living image of their idol at all costs. Yet, other scandals of the years between 1595 and the end of the 16th century are fully recorded in existing letters written by contemporaries. For instance, the Earl of Essex, favourite of Queen Elizabeth 1, had affairs with three of the Queen's maids of honour. These romances are mentioned in the letters, as is the enforced marriage of the Earl of Southampton when his lady-love was found to be pregant.

Thus, it can be seen that liaisons of the dangerous kind abounded in the naughty Nineties. It fact, it was regarded as quite normal for such dalliances to take place at court. Even today, should you wander along the passages of Hampton Court, you will see wall bars at which members of court used to rest to await an audience with the Queen or Cardinal Wolsey. But, if you ask the guide about these bars, he may tell you about their other use - as leaning posts for lovers.

Elizabeth's court was brimming with men and women in their late teens and twenties. They had little more to do than attend parties, balls and the theatre. They were more interested in having a good time than in boring court work. Indeed, but for the determination of Lord Salisbury and a few others, the court administration could well have collapsed. Even Elizabeth seemed to encourage the fun. It should not be forgotten that she was the daughter of Henry Tudor, whose womanising and visits to London's brothels are well documented. Some of the parties of those days went on for the best part of a week. There was food and drink aplenty and the young court crowd used to ride off into the "sticks" for a three or four-day spree before returning to London...for another party! It was one wild, social whirl.

The Queen filled her court with people who interested her, including personalities such as Sir Francis Drake and Sir Walter Raleigh, although I am not inferring that Drake and Raleigh were involved in the high jinks. Shakespeare was a different matter. He was not on the high seas or in some distant land. He was right there in the middle of all the glamour and gossip.

For their part, the women at court did more than merely decorate the scene. The Queen demanded that they be intellectually stimulating. One such person was a maid of honour called Mary Fitton. She was a popular choice as the Dark Lady for many years, but gave ground later to other candidates. For example, it was suggested that an innkeeper's wife, Mrs Devanante, from Oxford, was the woman in question, chiefly because one of her several children was named William and he became a poet. The boy studied at Oxford and wrote two or three tragedies, but none of note.

Another name put forward is that of Anne Whateley, or Whitely, who lived at Temple Grafton, near Stratford upon Avon. Shakespeare was said to have been courting her before Anne Hathaway came along and the poet dropped Mistress Whateley in a rush to marry Anne Hathaway because the latter was pregnant. Let us examine the claims of these women.

According to what we are told, Shakespeare, while making trips from Stratford to London, often called at an inn in the Cornmarket at Oxford. This inn, The Crown, was kept by a John Devanante, once a scholar of the Merchant Tailors School in London. He was a freeman of the company, says Sir Sidney Lee in his "The Life of William Shakespeare." He claims the mine host of The Crown was of a depressive disposition, whereas his wife was just the opposite, a beautiful extrovert, blonde and buxom.

She was the type of woman who might well have attracted gentlemen customers to the inn. Apart from Shakespeare, the Earl of Southampton and the Earl of Pembroke also found their way to The Crown. For John Devanante, it was his second marriage. His first, in 1591, was to an Anne Sackfeilde, of Bristol, who died childless. Then, some years later, he married Jane Shepherd, who came from Durham, and they had four sons and three daughters.

Shakespeare's frequent visits to the inn fostered personal friendship with the family and no doubt there was some local gossip when the fourth son came along because he was named William and the poet stood as his godfather. It is said that, years after, William Devanante was crossing The Common at Oxford when he bumped into one of the dons and knocked him over. The irate gentleman picked himself up and said: "William, why the hurry? What is the matter?" To this, the boy replied that his godfather was coming that day and bringing him many presents. The don, still annoyed, retorted: "Boy, do not take the name of the Lord God in vain."

Was this a cynical allusion to Shakespeare? Had rumours of a relationship reached his ears? Whether, in fact, William

Devanante was the result of a romance between Shakespeare and Mrs Devanante is impossible to say. But, given the promiscuous age in which the poet lived, I would be surprised if he rejected the opportunity of bedding the innkeeper's wife if she were as attractive as the contemporary writings would have us believe. Yet, she falls short of the mark when held up to scrutiny as a true contender for the title of the Dark Lady. A passing, enjoyable fancy perhaps, but not the all-consuming, passionate figure of mystery so powerfully described in the sonnets.

Anne Whateley, the illegitimate daughter of a Coventry woman, whose surname was Beck, and a much travelled Elizabethan, Anthony Jenkinson, of Market Harborough, Leicestershire, belonged to a religious teaching order and taught at a school for girls at Hillborough Manor, in the parish of Temple Grafton. It is said that it was here, in June, 1581, she met William. A year later, he took out a special licence to marry her, but we know the marriage never took place. Why?

For a long time now, there has been a debate about a recorded entry in the Bishop Worcester's register, issuing a licence authorising the marriage of a William Shaxpere and Anne Whateley, of Temple Grafton, on November 27, 1582. In that year, Shakespeare was 18 and Anne Whateley 21. The very next day, the same bishop's register records that a bond for the marriage of a William Shagspere and Anne Hathaway was applied for by Fulcone Sandells and John Rychardson, both of Stratford. They bonded themselves in the bishop's consistory court for a surety of £40 to free the bishop of all liability should a lawful impediment, by reason of any pre-contract, be disclosed.

We should not worry about the spelling of the surnames Shaxpere and Shagspere; Shakespeare's name was spelt in various ways. The question is: Did our young poet suddenly find himself in a marital mix-up? While courting Anne Whateley, was he also dallying with the older Anne Hathaway, who was seven years his senior? And, more to the point, what was the reason for the odd turn of events? Could it be that Anne Hathaway was pregnant?

Perhaps his indiscretions had caught up with him and he

was forced into a shotgun marriage. I subscribed to this view for many years, but my most recent research has raised doubts about this. First, however, let me refer to a newspaper report from the 19th century in which it is related that a certain Ignatius Donelly asserted the poet actually married Anne Whateley. The story was told to the Shakespeare Club, of Stratford, by a gentleman called Joseph Hill, from Perry Barr, Birmingham. Mr Hill said that, when the entry recording the licence was found in the bishop's register, "the doubters rose in the majesty of their strength and the claims of Shottery, which had lasted 300 years, were, to use their own words, 'more than threatened'; nay, he found some writers had invented a William Shakespeare, of Temple Grafton, to work the theory a little smoothly."

Mr Hill goes on to tell the august gathering at the Red Horse Hotel, Stratford, about the journey made by Shakespeare and the two "young friends", Fulcone Sandells and John Rychardson, to procure the licence from Worcester - three months after he had married Anne Hathaway! "There was not the smallest particle of doubt that the real marriage took place in August, 1582 and the ceremony in the church about 1st December following" (it was the custom of the time to wait a few months). But a William Shakespeare did take out a licence to marry an Anne Whateley - the records show it. So, was it the same William or could there be another explanation?

In his book, "The Life of William Shakespeare", Sir Sidney Lee expresses the opinion that the husband of Anne Whateley cannot be reasonably identified with the poet. Following my own research, I tend to agree - he was most probably another of the numerous William Shakespeares who lived in the diocese of Worcester which covered a wide area and was honeycombed with Shakespeare families of all degrees of gentility. The William Shakespeare whom Anne Whateley was licensed to marry was probably of a superior station, to which marriage by licence was deemed appropriate.

My investigation narrows down the area from where this other William Shakespeare may have come. In Rowington, some 10 miles north of Stratford, it was well known that between the 16th and 17th centuries, there were Shakespeares who lived at Shakespeare Hall, a half-timbered house occupied by John Richard Thomas and four William Shakespeares! The last William Shakespeare lived there around 1740 and there is reasonable evidence to assume that this family was connected with that of the poet. Therefore, the William Shakespeare who took out a special licence to marry Anne Whateley, of Temple Grafton, was, in all probability, not the poet but a kinsman of the same name from Rowington.

It is believed that Shakespeare's grandfather, Richard Shakespeare, moved from Wroxhall - which is a part of Rowington - to settle as a farmer in Snitterfield, four miles from Stratford, in 1535. He died in February, 1560, leaving goods and debts to his son, John, who was Shakespeare's father. John then left Snitterfield to seek a career at Stratford upon Avon.

During the course of my research, I obtained wills of the Shakespeare families of Rowington and Wroxhall from the Worcester archives. Among them were those of John Shakespeare (1574), Richard Shakespeare (1592), Joane Shaxper (1599), William Shakespeare (1599) and Thomas Shakespeare (1614). It appears, from translation of the wills, that most of them were farmers.

I also obtained the existing wills of the Whateley families. One family had lived at Stratford upon Avon, two at Wooton Wawan and the rest at Henley in Arden. None seemed to be connected with Anne Whateley, of Temple Grafton, but, in the printed parish register of Rowington and Wroxhall from 1616 to 1812, there is an entry from the bishop's transcript of 1629, under burials dated "20th Maie", about the "wief of William (Shaxpir)". Could this wife of William (Shakespeare?) have been Anne Whateley? Unfortunately, the woman's forename has been obliterated.

There are two pieces of documentary evidence which suggested that Richard Shaxpeare did, in fact, originate from Wroxhall and settle in Snitterfield. Ryland, in his "Records of Rowington", states that he translated a very interesting survey which appeared to be a tax return dated 1548. Richard Shaxpeare was mentioned as a visiting non-resident which suggests he was staying with kinsmen. Ryland also states that John Shakespeare, the poet's father, returned to Rowington in 1568 to serve as juror in a case concerning tithes of the manor house where his close friend, Hamnet Sadler, was a tenant. It is interesting to note that William Shakespeare named his only son, Hamnet, after his father's friend.

My research uncovered other wills and a bond of the Shakespeare families of Rowington and Wroxhall, as detailed here: bond, William Shakespeare, of Warwick (1579); will, William Shakespeare, of Wroxhall (1609); will, William Shakespeare, of Wroxhall (1612); will, William Shakespeare, July 11 (year lost); will, Richard Shaxpeare, weaver (1560); inventory, Richard Shaxpeare (1613); inventory, Richard Shaxpeare, of Rowington, the elder (year lost); and will, Richard Shaxpeare, the elder (1591).

The examination of these wills does not provide proof of relationship to the Stratford families, but strongly indicates that the majority were involved in agriculture. One Richard was a bailiff and one William a weaver. The reason for mentioning all these wills is to give an indication of the number of Shakespeares living in the area in the 16th and 17th centuries.

An examination of the bishop's transcript by the archivist at Worcester revealed that the portion of the page containing the burial entry referring to the wife of William (Shaxpir) has disappeared since Mr Ryland published his book in 1899-1900. Either it has been damaged in storage or torn off deliberately. This is very disappointing as the staff at the forensic laboratory in Birmingham said they were certain they could have revealed the obliterated name of the "wief" with their modern techniques.

There has been plenty of debate about which church William Shakespeare and Anne Hathaway chose for their marriage. Edmund Maloney's 1821 biography of the poet suggests they were wed at All Saints, Billesley, or the church of Weston upon Avon, near Luddington. Edgar Flower, who was chairman of the Shakespeare Birthplace Trust in early Victorian times, thought the poet was married in the small chapel at Luddington, but author R. B. Wheler, in his book about Stratford, said he had never heard of this belief; he said that, as far back as Malone's biography in 1798, Billesley was the most likely venue.

I took a team of investigators to Billesley in 1990 to explore the site and check out the theory. Groundscan, of Maidstone, did the radar surveys and the photography was by Optical Fibres, Olympus KMI, of Southend. The RAF Reconnaissance Unit, from Huntington, pitched in with aerial photography and I even had help from satellite photographs supplied by the National Remote Sensing Laboratory, at RAF Farnborough.

But, after considerable examination of all the information, all I was able to show was that the church did not appear to have a parish register for the relevant period. The computer centre of Leicester University, using variables, year, population and distance, rated the chances of a register in 1590 as only 0.42%, which was disappointing to say the least. So, the arguments still continue about where Shakespeare was married.

As a matter of interest, Anne Whateley died in 1600 at the age of 39 and may have been buried at Ashton, in Northamptonshire, or the chapel at Hillborough (this is the chapel of St Mary Magdelen which was pulled down in the Elizabethan period by John Huband). Although she is quite an intriguing figure, there are so many imponderables about Anne Whateley that she cannot be seriously considered as a Dark Lady candidate.

Another contender sometimes put forward is Lucy Morgan, otherwise known as Black Lucy, of Clerkenwell, or Lucy negro-abbess de Clerkenwell. A negress and a prostitute, she ran a brothel frequented by the court's gentry and the argument in her favour is the colour of her skin, thus a dark lady. It is also known that she was at Hampton Court, if only for a year. A document in the Records Office, in London, reveals that she was a servant at the palace from 1581 to 1582 and that, on a particular occasion, received a sum of 6s 8d. For what, we do not know, although her later activities may give us a clue. But I dismiss her from the list because we are seeking a gifted intellectual and a companion of the Queen, not a servant girl who became a brothel keeper.

Mary Fitton was the first of the Dark Lady contenders for several reasons, mainly because so much was known about her. She had striking looks, she was tall and she was intelligent - and she soon became a firm favourite at Elizabeth's court.

There is a painting of her aged 15, two years before she entered court, another picture at the aged of 18 and yet a third when she is seen in procession a few steps behind the Queen, leading the ladies-in-waiting. There are love letters written about her, addressed to her elder sister, Anne, and she is probably referred to in Shakespeare's "Love Labour's Lost" when the word "fit" is used in the form or an apparent pun (act IV, scene 1, line 145) - it was fashionable at the time to apply double meanings to names and words. Another instance of this can be seen on the tablet of one of the monuments to the Fittons in parish church at Gawsworth, Cheshire. The inscription reads: "Whose solve's and Body's beauties sentence them Fit ones to wear a heavenly Diadem."

Thomas Tyler, in "The Herbert-Fitton Theory", emphasises that the name Fitton was taken contemporaneously to mean "fit one". This is further illustrated in sonnet 51 when Shakespeare talks of his "triumphant prize" which been interpreted to allude to Mary Fitton's high position as a maid of honour. If we look at the phrase with the knowledge that puns were popular, we can see that innuendo and suggestion were the keywords of the day and who better at manipulating the English language than Shakespeare himself?

Letters written by courtiers of the late 16th century may have disappeared, but the greatest evidence of all concerning the bard's involvement in a sex triangle is contained in his sonnets, which provide clues to the identities of the Dark Lady and Fair Youth without actually naming them. Sprinkled throughout the lines of these 154 items of verse are intimations of romantic dalliances.

Sonnets 1 to 126 tell how Shakespeare loved a youth of rank and beauty, whereas the remainder of the sonnets concern an overwhelming infatuation with an attractive woman. The two sets of sonnets are bound together by a story which is told in both - how the Fair Youth was seduced by the Dark Lady and how Shakespeare forgave the boy, but was tormented by the treachery of the Dark Lady.

In sonnet 20, we read:

"A woman's face, with Nature's own hand painted
Has thou, the master-mistress of my passion:
A woman's gentle heart, but not acquainted
With shifting change, as is false women's fashion;
An eye more bright than theirs, less false in rolling,
Gilding the object whereupon it gazeth;
A man in hue, all 'hues' in his controlling,
Which steals men's eyes and women's souls amazeth.
And for a woman wert thou first created;
Till Nature as she wrought thee, fell a-doting"

Later in the same sonnet:

"Mine be thy love, and thy love's use their treasure."

What clearer picture could one require than this of a loving address to an effeminate man?

Shakespeare even says how long the relationship lasted with his young "master-mistress". Sonnet 104 opens by telling his "fair friend" that:

"You never can be old,
For as you were when first your eye I eyed,
Such seems your beauty still."

Then he adds:

"Three April perfumes in three hot Junes burn'd,
Since first I saw you fresh, which yet are green."

So, they had been close for at least three years. But, what of the Dark Lady? Sonnet 135 relates:

"Whoever hath her wish, thou hast thy 'Will,'
And 'Will' to boot and 'Will' in overplus;"

Shakespeare was clearly smitten by the lady's charms and

certain scholars suggest the reference to "Will" means his sexual prowess.

Sonnet 136 continues the story:

"Will will fulfil the treasure of thy love,
Ay, fill it full with wills, and my will one...
Make but my name thy love, and love that still,
And then thou lovest me for my name is Will."

Dewy-eyed words, indeed, but the tone of the ode changes dramatically in sonnet 137:

"If eyes, corrupt by over-partial looks,
Be anchor'd in the bay where all men ride,
Why of eyes' falsehood hast thou forged hooks,
Whereto the judgement of my heart is tied?"

The word "ride" has obvious sexual connotations and the final line of this damning verse goes:

"And to this false plague are they now transferred."

"Plague" in this context means mistress. Therefore, it can be appreciated that Shakespeare was fully aware that he was not the only man in the Dark Lady's love life, not by any means. However, if any further confirmation is required that the poet endured two intensely passionate affairs, sonnet 144 reveals:

"Two loves I have, of comfort and despair,,
Which like two spirits do suggest me still;
The better angel is a man right fair,
The worser spirit a woman colour'd ill.
To win me soon to hell, my female evil
Tempteth my better angel from my side,
And would corrupt my saint to be a devil,
Wooing his purity with her foul pride."

There we have it - a love for a man and a woman. The sonnets indicate that he found the company of the man more agreeable than that of the woman and he leaves one in no doubt that he had scant regard for the Dark Lady's wiles in tempting away his "right fair" angel.

Sonnet 134 confirms:

"Him have I lost, thou has both him and me:
He pays the whole, and yet am I not free."

Then, in sonnet 147:

"For I have sworn thee fair, and thought thee bright,
Who art as black as hell, as dark as night."

It could be argued that Shakespeare is expressing his anger here at his young friend whom he described as a man "right fair," but following the tirade of sonnet 144, it is clear that the literary dagger is aimed at the corrupting woman's heart. First, Shakespeare met the Fair Youth, with whom he formed a relationship of "comfort." Then, after at least three years of companionship with the youth, the poet became entangled with a woman...only for her to steal away the youth. Later, her relationship with Shakespeare was ended by the poet because of her treachery.

But, you may ask, why did Shakespeare risk his reputation at court and in the land by writing such intimate passages? The answer is simple: the sonnets were never intended for publication. They may have been passed around a small circle of close friends but it is not even certain that the principals in the saga saw what he had written about them. The sonnets were Shakespeare's own private views, probably written while alone, jotted down as one would in a diary while the drama unfolded. Compiled over a five-year period between 1594 and 1599, they were eventually acquired by Thomas Thorpe who published them in 1609, seven years before Shakespeare's death. It is not known how Thorpe managed to get his hands on them. They could have been stolen or one of Shakespeare's literary associates may have betrayed him. Whatever happened, it must have come as a terrible shock to the poet when they were published.

CHAPTER 2

The maid Mary

"Curiosity in the case of this bewitching and tormenting creature can hardly be avoided by readers who are swept along on the waves of Shakespeare's impassioned surrender to her sovereign charms and of his furious rebellion against her lascivious and treacherous behaviour." - Ivor Brown: The Women in Shakespeare's Life, 1968.

The Dark Lady is, without doubt, one of the most fascinating seductresses in literature. At the splendid court of Queen Elizabeth I, filled with scores of the most aristocratic women, it appears that, for a few years at least, the Dark Lady outshone them all.

The majority of literary scholars and historians admit the existence of the Dark Lady, but they cannot agree on her identity. Indeed, some maintain that her identity will never be known. We shall see ....

The disagreement over the candidates was caused partly by the fact that her description in the sonnets fitted several ladies at the Elizabethan court. There were many who flirted with members of the circle of the Earls of Essex, Southampton and Pembroke. They also took poets as lovers and, thus, made the identity of the Dark Lady even more difficult to establish.

Among the more persistent champions of Mary Fitton's claims were Professor Tyler, of Imperial College, London, George Bernard Shaw and Frank Harris. Professor Tyler's book was published in 1886 and he was convinced she had black hair. Bernard Shaw revived Tyler's book and became a

Fittonite for a while. In his short play, "The Dark Lady of the Sonnets", the heroine is Mary.

Frank Harris, who was her most fanatical supporter, wrote in his "The Man Shakespeare": "Shakespeare owed a great part of his renown to Mary Fitton." He added in "The Women of Shakespeare" (1911): "This woman dominated all Shakespeare's maturity...and changed him from a light-hearted writer of comedies, histories and songs into the greatest man who has left record of himself in literature."

The arguments about Mary's hair colour were revived after the publication of a book by Lady Newdigate, a Victorian, who was also the wife of a descendent of Mary's sister, Anne Fitton. She uncovered in the muniment (document) room of her ancestral home, Arbury Hall, a collection of letters to Anne by various courtiers about Mary's downfall, disgrace and banishment from court. They formed the basis of the book, published in 1897 under the title "Gossip from a Muniment Room, being passages in the lives of Anne and Mary, 1574-1618."

Lady Newdigate refuted Professor Tyler's assertions that Mary had black hair. She said that, on her surviving portraits at the hall, Mary had brown hair, a fair complexion and grey eyes. This news silenced Tyler and his followers; they were not about to challenge the word of a lady, particularly when the key evidence hung in her home. However, those who obtained a copy of Lady Newdigate's book were somewhat surprised to see the reproductions of Mary's portraits showing her with distinctly dark hair. This, of course, could have been over-inking in the printing!

Ivor Brown, author of several excellent books on Shakespeare, wrote about this in "The Women in Shakespeare's Life." He said: "Any reader of the Muniment Gossip book, confronted with the portraits as reproduced, could swear that here is the Dark Lady 'as black as hell, as dark as night'."

I resolved, after all this confusion, to see for myself what was the colour of Mary's hair when one of her portraits was put on view at an exhibition in 1972. This was "The Masque of Beauty" exhibition at the National Portrait Gallery in London and the country's most famous beauties of the last

400 years were on the walls. One of the pictures, as I said, was of Mary; it was from the collection at Lady Newdigate's home - and it showed Mary as an attractive brunette.

According to experts, the portrait was painted by an artist belonging to the circle of George Gower on or around 1595. The catalogue, in addition to listing details of her life, added that she was "at one time considered to be Shakespeare's Dark Lady." I should mention here, just to confuse the issue about the hair colour, that another picture of Mary hangs at Sherborne Castle in Dorset. This shows the maid Mary and Queen Elizabeth, the latter on a portable throne, in procession. And this picture has Mary with raven-black hair!

I sometimes wonder if Lady Newdigate was a little selective with the truth. One picture did, indeed, show that Mary had brown hair. But there was no mention of the other picture in which she appears with hair "as dark as night". Perhaps Tyler and his supporters would not have gone away so quickly if they had known; still, one can speculate that, at least, the spotlight was removed from the Fitton name after Lady Newdigate's interjection and that, no doubt, pleased the family.

Portrait of Mary Fitton
... believed by Arthur Marlowe to be the Dark Lady of Shakespeare's sonnets

(Reproduced by permission of the trustees of the Newdigate Settlement)

One other view in this debate is worth recording. Clara Longworth de Chambrun, in her "Shakespeare", dismissed Mary Fitton as the Dark Lady in a footnote which says: "The gay and pretty Mary Fitton was fair with green eyes, while the author of the sonnets declares that his mistress was married and brunette with black eyes."

Well, I have already demonstrated that Mary did not have fair hair, and, in fact, the sonnets do not say the Dark Lady was married; they accuse her of being "false to a bed-vow". Could this not mean she had sworn to Shakespeare that he was her only lover and he made the accusation after he discovered she had broken this vow by sleeping with others? She did not have to be married at all. Clara Longworth de Chambrun also reveals that someone in the last century tampered with a manuscript in the Bodleian Library; it was about the poet's indiscretion with the wife of an innkeeper (Mrs Devanante?)

Both in the sonnets and the plays, Shakespeare dwells on the same dark beauty emphasising her physical attributes. In Romeo and Juliet, he describes Rosaline, Romeo's first love, in unnecessary detail considering she never appears in the play! The description fits the Dark Lady of the sonnets (and Mary Fitton) in every respect. There is no reason or theatrical excuse for such close portraiture.

Ivor Brown again: "The only explanation is the dramatist's obsession. The idea of a lecherous beauty brings the image of one such actual woman bursting out of his subconscious self with the exactitude of colour photography. The play was written the year Mistress Fitton came to London."

The plays describe the Dark Lady at several stages of Shakespeare's love for her. In Romeo and Juliet, the spotlight is on a young girl, at first adored from a distance. Later, there is another image, more intimate, inspired by the brief period when Shakespeare felt she loved him, and only him. Finally, there is the "lecherous beauty".

The same lady, again called Rosaline, is more kindly treated in Love's Labour's Lost, but there was an earlier version of the play which omitted the fawning description of the amorous Rosaline. The quarto edition of 1598 states: "A Pleasant Conceited Comedie called Love's Labour's Lost as it was presented before Her Highness this last Christmas ... newly corrected and augmented by W. Shakespeare." I find it intriguing that the poet should have changed the text before the royal command performance during Christmas, 1597.

By that time, Mary Fitton had been at court for more than two years. As one of the maids of honour, she would have been present on the royal occasion and would have heard the allusions to herself and two Wills in her life (Shakespeare and William Herbert, the Earl of Pembroke). Was Rosaline introduced to spite Mary after the poet discovered she was having an affair with Pembroke?

Shakespeare may have "augmented" several plays with Mary in mind. The most cruel was in Twelfth Night, enacted shortly after her disgrace in January, 1601. "Mall" Fitton was then seven months pregnant with the Earl of Pembroke's child and already banished from court (she gave birth to a short-lived son in February or March, 1601). Her disgrace was public knowledge and the painting depicting her at the side of the Queen on her processional throne had been removed from the palace wall.

In act 1, scene 5, Sir Andrew Ague-cheek boasts of his many accomplishments. Sir Toby Belch replies: "Wherefore are these things hid? Are they like to take dust like Mistress Mall's picture?" If this were an allusion to Mary Fitton, the audience of courtiers must have enjoyed this topical joke. Burning with fury, the betrayed poet appears to have taken his revenge through the power of the quill.

If Mary were nothing but a superficial acquaintance of Shakespeare's, would the chivalrous and sensitive writer have referred to her in such a brutally inconsiderate fashion? Surely not, but if she were the "lascivious and treacherous" Dark Lady who seduced the Fair Youth and hurt his sexual vanity, then it is understandable that the betrayed lover felt compelled to vent his wrath in such a manner.

Returning to the sonnets, I find it curious that none were discovered among the documents and correspondence so carefully preserved by Mary Fitton's sister, Anne, the first Lady Newdigate. That Mary's lover, the Earl of Pembroke, was one of Shakespeare's friends and benefactors is fully documented. So is the fact that Mary was at court when, according to contemporary evidence, the manuscripts of the sonnets were circulated there.

Two questions arise from this: Is it likely that Anne never had a copy from her sister or from her friends at court? Is it plausible that Anne did not preserve a single "muniment" to the Dark Lady? To me, it would seem that Anne, if she had possessed any of these, would not have given a thought to the possibility that her descendents might be embarrassed by them. Nevertheless, in the Newdigate family archives that survived intact until the end of the 19th century, the writer of the "Gossip from a Muniment Room" did not find anything of such a nature.

After the early death of her illegitimate son, Mary returned to Cheshire where she did not mend her ways. According to Sir Peter Leycester, a Cheshire gentleman of those days, Mary had two illegitimate daughters by a friend of her family, Admiral Sir Richard Leveson.

Some historians believe this might have been malicious libel, although it is a fact that another nautical gentleman, Captain Polewheele, married her in great haste, just before, or just after, the birth of a son.

The Fitton family seat was at Gawsworth Manor, an imposing, half-timbered house in the village of Gawsworth, Cheshire. We know a few details of the history of the manor, but no original print of its structure has been found. What visitors see today is only part of the building, an L-shaped outline, standing in 18 acres of lawns and gardens. There is a tradition that, in the 17th century, the library and studies were destroyed in a fire; the other theory is that the Victorians, in their zeal for restoration, pulled down the walls and then tried to reconstruct the building.

I favour the former as the most likely occurrence; that is, the house caught fire accidentally, or intentionally, around the year 1657. Of course, if it were accidental, there is no more to be said, but if it were otherwise, there must have been a strong motive. We know the Fittons were an unusual family and mystery accompanied them throughout the years they resided at Gawsworth. Is it stretching credibility too far to suggest they might have burned down the house themselves? Why? To destroy valuable documents which would have got into the hands of the Roundheads who were on the rampage at the height of the Civil War? Or, did enemies of the family deliberately set fire to the manor? After all, Commonwealth troops looted and burned the homes of Royalist families.

I think it quite possible that, in the Civil War, Gawsworth Manor contained a number of important state papers in the library and studies; there may even have been some original work by William Shakespeare. Perhaps, even, the sonnets written to Mary Fitton were kept in safety and, rather than let them and the house fall prey to the Roundheads, the family set the building alight. In that case, the remains of the manor are the result of the actions of Cromwell's men or the villagers' efforts to save the house and its contents.

I acquired from the then Ministry of Housing and Local Government aerial photographs of Gawsworth taken in a survey by the Royal Air Force. On examination, the photographs showed markings on the right of the manor indicating an ornamental pond that was there 200 years ago. More to the south west was what looked like the original 1395 site of Gawsworth Manor. To the west, there was a mound some 650 feet in length called the tilting ground.

Many a scene of knightly feats must have been enacted there. It is believed the Fittons used a tilting ground until the end of the 16th century. Around 1575, Sir Edward was sent to Ireland on court business and he took with him his wife, Lady Alice. While they were in Munster, Mary Fitton was born in 1578 and shortly afterwards the family returned to Cheshire, as shown by the parish register at Gawsworth which records Mary's baptism on June 24,1578. She had two brothers and a sister older than herself.

The next entry in the register concerning the Fittons is of the marriage of Mary's sister, Anne, when she was 14 to John Newdigate, of Arbury Hall, near Nuneaton. At 17, Mary was taken to London to become maid of honour to Queen Elizabeth and was left in the care of Sir William Knollys, a friend of the Fittons and Elizabeth's Controller of Court.

Sir William was married to a much older woman and, from the letters written by him to Anne Fitton, it is clear that he became infatuated with his ward. Knollys, in fact, had quite a reputation with the ladies; at night, he was often to be seen tripping from his bedroom to the quarters of the maids which were situated conveniently close by.

At court, Mary soon gained favour in the eyes of the Queen. Note the following passage in a letter from Rowland Whyte to Sir Robert Sidney: "There is to be a memorable masks of eight ladies. They have a strange dawnce newly invented, their attire is this: each hath a skirt of cloth of silver, a rich waist-coat wrought with silks and gold and silver, a mantell of carnacion taffeta cast under their arms, and their hair loose about their shoulders curiously knotted and interlaced. These are the Maskers, My Lady Dority Hastings, Mistress Fitton, Mistress Carey, Mistress Onslow and My Lady Blanche Somersett. These eight dawnce to the music Apollo brings, and there is a fine speech that mentions of a ninth, much to her Honor and Praise."

And, in another letter written shortly afterwards: "After supper, the masks come in, and delicate it was to see eight ladies soe prettily and richly attired. Mistress Fitton leads, and after they had donne all their own ceremonies, these eight ladies maskers choose eight ladies more to dawnce the measure. Mistress Fitton went to the Queen and woed her to dawnce. Her Majestie asked who she was: 'Affection' she said. 'Affection' said the Queen, 'Affection is false'. Yet her Majestie rose and dawnced, so did my Lady Marques."

The portrait, "Queen Elizabeth borne in Procession", which I have already mentioned, presents a puzzle. The maid of honour, generally believed to be Mary, is in the foreground of the picture, demonstrating how prominent she had become in court. By her side is a gentleman with whom she appears to he holding hands. Is this the Earl of Pembroke? As we now know, their affair resulted in Mary's banishment from court.

And why was the maid Mary wearing the blazing heart sign of "Affection" on her sleeve - the same sign as that on the sleeve of the Queen's gown? It was very rare for people to wear the same emblem. Mary must have occupied an exalted position in the eyes of the Queen who, letters show, displayed her "Affection" by presenting Mary with a horse as a personal gift. Did Mary feel she was so popular with the Queen that she could even get away with holding hands with one of her lovers?

Apart from Pembroke, who was a leading contender for the Fair Youth title with many an historian, the Earls of

Southampton and Essex were other conquests in Mary's life. It is inferred that she was married while at court and there is also the following letter, again from Rowland Whyte to Sir Robert Sidney, in 1600: "One Mistress Martin who dwelt at the Chopinge Knife near Ludgate tould me yt she hath see ne priests mary gentlewomen at the Court, in that tyme when that Mistress Fitton was in great favour, and one of her Majestie's maids of honour, and duringe the tyme yt the Earle of Pembroke favord her she would put off her tire and tucke upp her clothes and take a large white cloake and march as though she had bene a man to meete the said Earle out of the Courts."

Mary was risking her position at court and the esteem in which she was held by the Queen by continuing her association with Pembroke – a daring affair, indeed, if we are to believe she disguised herself as a man before sneaking out of the palace to meet him. As it was, the couple engineered their own downfall through the inevitable sequel to their excursions when, in 1601, Mary was found to be pregnant. The earl was questioned and admitted to being the father, although he renounced all claims of marriage and left Mary literally holding the baby.

A letter from Sir Robert Cecil to Sir George Carew demonstrates how seriously the matter was viewed: "We have no news but that there is a misfortune befallen Mistress Fytton, for she is proved with child, and the Earl of Pembroke being examined confesseth a fact but utterly renounceth all marriage. I fear that they will both dwell in the Tower awhile for the Queen hath vowed to send them thither." As it turned out, the Queen's anger was tempered by her regard for Mary and her condition (she was about five months pregnant) and, in the end, only banished her from court.

Pembroke, however, was not so fortunate. A letter at the Public Records Office, London, discloses: "The Earl of Pembroke is committed to the Fleet (prison). His cause is delivered of a boy who is dead." Pembroke was in prison for a few months before being released and, after things had quietened down, eventually married into respectability.

Meanwhile, Mary had lost her love, her court career was

in tatters and her child was dead. It must have been a heart-breaking time and she sought solace in her family and friends. Most of them stood by her, but not her mother, Lady Alice, later to be Dame Alice Fitton. She was disgusted by it all and would not have her daughter in the house at Gawsworth.

Mary's father, was more forgiving. A rather naive letter from Sir Edward to Sir Robert Cecil, dated May 16, 1601, reads:

"I can say nothing of the erle but my daughter is confident in her chance before God and wishethe my Lo and she might be meet before in different senes. But for myself I expect no good from hyme that in all this tyme hath not shewed any kindness. I count my daughter as good a gentlewoman as my Lo is though her dignity (be greater onlye in him) wch hathe begiled her I ffeare, except my Los honesty bee the greater vertuoes."

The tone of that letter contrasts sharply with a note from Lady Alice to her other daughter, Anne, in which she says: "I take no joye to heer of your sister. If it hade plesed God when I did bear her that she and I hade bine beried it hade saved mee from a great delle of sorow and gryffe, and her from shame and such shame as never hade Chessyre woman, worse now than ever."

During all this time, Sir William Knollys was writing reams of letters about Mary to Anne, generally bewailing the fact that she had passed over his "loving" care. From these letters, we deduce that Mary went to stay with Anne at Arbury Hall while the court scandal died down. On the surface, at least, it was an ideal move. Yet, in many ways, Anne was not unlike her more celebrated sister. She tempted courtiers into her home, particularly Francis Beaumont, scholar and gentleman, and "Cousin Saunders".

Francis, afterwards master at Charterhouse, was a keen suitor of Anne's, in addition to being a warm advocate of the rival admirer, "Cousin Saunders", who was actually Matthew Saunders, son of William Saunders, of Welford, in Northamptonshire. Francis was the second son of Nicholas Beaumont, of Coleorton, in Leicestershire, and Anne was the daughter of William Saunders, the younger brother of Francis.

Matthew courted Anne for several years although, being somewhat shy, he asked Francis to write his love letters! Odd, yes, but in reality, a shrewd idea because Francis was noted for his writing and oratory. Matthew was called "Cousin", by the way, to conceal his identity in case the love letters were intercepted. This would have been undesirable as he was in line for a knighthood, which he received in 1617, six years before his death.

After a while, Francis became so wrapped up in his pages of passion that he fell in love with Anne, as well. So the two friends became rival suitors.

Francis then made his big mistake in consulting Mary Fitton about Anne's affections. Little did he realise that Matthew had been Mary's consort for some time, as proved by Lady Newdigate's book, in which it states that Matthew occasionally discussed with Mary how best to advance his suit.

Mary was a woman who did not permit anyone to benefit through her for no return, so we can safely assume that she gained something from Matthew. It was not cash, because he did not have a great deal, and it was not land, because he did not have much of that, either. Could it have been love? I think, knowing Mary, that this was the reward she demanded in return for advancing Matthew's claims with her sister.

Francis, on the other hand, was not prepared to be blackmailed in any way, shape or form. The only thing he had going for him was his ardent admiration expressed so lovingly in his letters. That was not enough, however, and we can imagine that Mary was not slow in putting down the poison whenever she talked with her sister about Francis.

It is interesting to note that on the back of one of Anne's letters she made a rough copy of an answer she wanted to send to Francis. She implied that he was impudent and had a mischievous tongue and, further, if his conversation was anything like his letters, then she would expect little peace from him. The sarcasm was not one-sided. In a letter from Francis to Anne, he writes: "Ever since I last saw your Ladyship, I have been with my dying pelican (by this, he means Saunders) where I have wrought a miracle in somewhat reviving dead affections that lay buried for years, seven foot within the earth under a dead body."

The "dead body" was Matthew Saunders' first wife who died in 1605. Her maiden name was Anne Skipworth and she lived near to the village of Shangton, in Leicestershire. She died quite young, leaving four children. With nothing going right for him in the romance stakes, Francis eventually accepted defeat and quit the chase.

But, according to Lady Newdigate, the path of true love did not run smoothly. Despite the fact that Mary had laid the table for the game of courtship to begin, and also that they knew each other for eight years after his wife's death, Matthew was unable to persuade Anne to marry him. Mary, again, up to her tricks in the background?

We do not know the reason, but there is no doubt that finally, rejected, Matthew returned to Shangton to a life of solitude in his manor. That would have been the end of the affair, had it not been for another of those tantalising puns which keep cropping up about the Fitton name. At the time of his break-up with Anne, in 1612, Matthew erected a plaque on the chancel wall of his manor. Experts have regarded it as an epitaph to his wife, but was it ...? The words read:

"How should respectless death so rightly hit, those whose perfection they of this world from failing,
Does not heaven's mercy choose the only FIT to inherit;
Lest forever by their challenge you in whose breasts lives any spark of good, •
Pass not without compassion when you view how poor a deal of earth, or stone, or wood covers all goodness
And shall once cover you."

When I saw the word "fit" on the plaque, I was immediately reminded of the Fittons. Was this an epitaph from a grief-stricken husband to his dead wife? Or, was it a tablet to the memory of his other love, Anne Fitton? The latter is more likely when one considers that the inscription was cut seven years after his wife died.

CHAPTER 3

The W.H. mystery

The arguments still rage about the identity of "the onlie begetter" of the sonnets, Mr W.H., but I believe he was well known in the Elizabethan period and by no means a mystery to Shakespeare's acquaintances.

His circle of associates were poets, artists, men of letters and intellectuals, so it is almost certain that Mr W.H. would have been a man of high intellect and quite possibly a poet himself. He would have been a theatregoer but was not, I maintain, the third Earl of Pembroke, William Herbert, as commonly thought.

It has been assumed in the past that, because he was one of the dedicatees of the First Folio, he must have been Shakespeare's Fair Youth. Pembroke, as we have seen, was one of Mary Fitton's lovers and, no doubt, he was on friendly terms with Shakespeare. That was to be expected as the poet had gained favour with Elizabeth and, unless you wished to antagonise the Queen, it was wise to go along with her tastes in people.

Further, and, to my mind, conclusively, one would not address an earl of the realm as plain "Mr.", not even Shakespeare. To do so was unheard of. Previous researchers attempted to dismiss this from their minds. They tried to explain glibly, but not convincingly, that William Herbert must have been the Fair Youth - he was a patron, his initials fitted, everything was right. Except, of course, that he was an earl.

That uncomfortable fact was swept under the carpet and the "experts" proceeded merrily along, certain that the mystery of the Fair Youth had been solved. It did not ring true to me, however, and when I had the good fortune to acquire a number of wills of the Fitton family from the Probate Registry in London, I set about exploring the doubts in my mind.

There were 15 wills in all, comprising 70 pages, and they were translated for me by a Mr Chinnery of the Department of Archives in Leicester Museum. After wading through about half of them, I came to the will of Francis Fitton, who was the brother of Mary's father. He died in 1608, although his will was made about six years earlier.

It is a massive document, consisting of eight pages, but hidden among the numerous paragraphs was the chink of light for which I had been searching. The passage read: "1 leave certain writings and books meant for no-one else's eyes but my dear friend William Herbert, son of Sir Edward Herbert, deceased. William Herbert now Knight."

Over the next few months, I made enquiries in various archives, at the Probate Registry again, and from other sources, in an attempt to gain more information about this knight, but without success. It began to look as though he had disappeared off the face of the earth without a trace, until, almost in desperation, I contacted the Leicester Reference Library.

I asked for information about William Herbert from "The Official Baronetcy of England, from 1066 to 1855" by J Doyle. What a stroke of luck this had proved to be, for in one of the pages was contained the following: "William Herbert the first, grandson of William, first Earl of Pembroke, Baron of Powis, born about 1573. He was made a Knight of the Bath, July 23rd 1603. He was made a Chancellor Wales 1608 and created Baron of Powis, April 2nd 1629."

There were other details about him, but perhaps the most striking of all was the information at the foot of the page: William Herbert had married Lady Eleanor Percy, the third daughter of Henry, eighth Earl of Northumberland, before 1600.

This is crucial to our search for Mr W.H. because we already know that, when the eighth earl died, Francis Fitton married his widow. So, here is the proof that the William

Herbert called "my dear friend" by Francis Fitton in his will was the same man mentioned in the book I read in the reference library at Leicester. It should be noted that William Herbert was not created a knight until July 23,1603; that means we have a Mr. William Herbert close to the Fitton family when the sonnets were written between 1594 and 1599.

Pembroke was alive, too, but he was an earl. In other words, there were two William Herberts. I was later to learn that an earlier discoverer of this man was Ulric Nisbet ("The Onlie Begetter", 1936); my entirely independent investigation was conducted in 1968 while at Loughborough University.

But what caused the mix-up which led to the Earl of Pembroke being awarded the Fair Youth accolade? Mr William Herbert was the son of Sir Edward Herbert and the grandson of the first Earl of Pembroke. The other William Herbert, the earl, was the son of Henry, who was Sir Edward's brother.

Mr. W.H. is a mystery no longer. At the time of the sonnets (1594), "Mr" William Herbert was 21 and Shakespeare 30. Mr W.H. was known as William Herbert of the Red Castle, Montgomeryshire and he was made the first Lord Powys in 1629.

The London and Middlesex Society Journal states: "William (his eldest son) was made a Knight of the Bath at the Coronation of King James the First, and departed this life upon the 7th day of March, 1655, was buried at Hendon, County Middlesex, with the epitaph."

The librarian who had been helping me showed me a book, which I think was an offshoot of the Middlesex Journal. This included a surprising passage: "Dorney Court, Buckinghamshire. Extracts from the Parish Register. William Herbert, Lord of Powis, was buried the 21st day of June, 1656." So, 16 months after being buried at Hendon, William Herbert was re-interred at Dorney Court, Buckinghamshire. Why?

I wrote to the vicar at Dorney Vicarage who put me in touch with Miss Sheila Oakley, to whom I am indebted. She went to great lengths to find out more about this man. About the same time, I wrote to Buckinghamshire County Council Archives Department, who were most helpful. My last letter to them, however, brought further disappointment.

It read: "I can confirm that the Dorney Parish Records have recently been deposited here. However, one of the early registers is evidently missing, and there is a gap in the burials between 1645 and 1726."

Talk about bad luck. I seemed to be plagued with papers having been destroyed during the Civil War and people, either incompetent or wanting to hide something, losing parish registers. This misfortune, however, was followed by news from Miss Oakley which stated: "In 1625 he (James Palmer) married Catharine, 16 years his junior, widow of Sir Robert Vaughan of Llwydiarth of Llangedwyn Hall in Montgomery.

"She was the daughter of Sir William Herbert KB, created First Baron of Powis Castle, Montgomeryshire."

I can only speculate on the reason why her father's remains were transferred to Dorney Court. The Palmer family has lived in the manor at Dorney for hundreds of years. His daughter had been married to Sir James Palmer for 30 years when her father died and was buried at Hendon. At the time, Lady Catherine Palmer probably thought it would be a good idea to have her father buried at Dorney Court.

The delay between the two burials was almost certainly due to administration within the two dioceses concerned. But whether her father was interred in the Palmer family vault in St. James' Church, Dorney, or whether his daughter had a special small vault built for him - which would also account for some of the delay - is not known. Certainly, there is no indication in the church, no monument, no plaque, to say that Sir William Herbert KB, First Lord of Powys, is buried there.

Efforts on my part to obtain permission from the present member of the Palmer family to enter the vault have failed. It would have been a fitting conclusion to have been able to establish that William Herbert is actually in the Palmer family vault. Nevertheless, I have demonstrated William Herbert was known to Francis Fitton, Mary's favourite uncle. That means he almost certainly met Mary - and that puts him close to Shakespeare.

Which brings me back to the man himself. It is a puzzle to me, like everyone else, why so few facts about the bard's life have been recorded; it would be wonderful if one day a "lost" sonnet turned up in a vault (I hope I'm there if it does!). But, as it stands today, we have to turn to the well established sources to set down exactly what is known. April was his month, of that there is no little doubt. He was born on or around April 23,1564 and was buried on April 25,1616, aged 52.

He was the third child of John Shakespeare and Mary Arden; she was the daughter of Robert Arden who lived at Wilmcote. William was baptised, it is believed, on April 26, three days after his birth. Shakespearian scholar, George Stevens, adopted the April 23 birthday in his 1773 edition of Shakespeare. It was the tradition in those days to allow three days to elapse between birth and baptism. Some academics insist he must have gone to university to gain his skill with the language, but I think he developed a natural talent at the local grammar school and, through his interest in the theatre in later years, honed it to the level of perfection we now admire.

The lost years in Shakespeare's life, as scholars like to call them, occurred between the age of 15, when it is believed he left school, and his arrival in London. By the age of 21, he was at the home of the Southampton family. Countless explanations have been put forward about what Shakespeare might have been doing during those years. Teaching is one suggestion; another is that he was a private tutor to a Catholic family.

The biographer Rowe, whose writings were drawn from statements and anecdotes collected by the actor, Betterton, in early 18th century Stratford, says Shakespeare received a meagre education at the grammar school in Stratford, learning the basics of Latin before joining his father in his business as a "considerable dealer in wool". But Malone, another historian, says the story that Shakespeare learned only the basics of Latin was put about to suit a theory that he showed an "ignorance of the ancients" in his plays.

In fact, it is stated in the English Cyclopaedia of the 19th century that the free school of Stratford, founded in the reign of Henry VI, was under the direction of men who, as university graduates, were qualified to "diffuse that sound scholarship which was once the boast of England". So, it seems, Shakespeare's education was thorough enough.

Schools in the provinces taught the "Old English" style of writing and Shakespeare's handwriting shows he used this type of script. Pupils studied Latin and were well versed in the works of Virgil, Circero and Horace. French, too, was popular and young William seems to have learned the language as indicated by lengthy French dialogue in scenes from Henry V.

His father took William away from school at an early age. He was about 13 when he began helping in the wool business, which was suffering at the time. Perhaps it was his father's financial difficulties that persuaded him to try to steal a deer from Sir Thomas Lucy's park at Charlecote, near Stratford. The youngster was caught and Sir Thomas brought a prosecution against him. William is reputed to have written a stinging ballad about the gentleman - and paid for it by having his fine doubled!

The youth did not stay much longer in Stratford; apparently he thought there was a better way of earning a living than dealing in wool.

Personally, I think young William's fascination for the strolling players, who often visited Stratford and the surrounding district, lured him away from his family. He would have grabbed every opportunity to watch the performances of these players; can you imagine the effect this would have had on a boy whose sole pleasure in life was the theatrical profession? The theory I offer is that he simply joined one of the groups of players when they were at Stratford, possibly to the dismay of his parents.

This can be understood, for in those days strolling players were classed as vagabonds, tramps and scoundrels. But, to Shakespeare, they represented a fascinating way of life. He had found what he wanted to do; he grasped the opportunity with both hands and joined their ranks. One can well imagine those next two or three years as he travelled about

England with the players, presenting their plays to the people in the towns and villages where entertainment was rare and there was little for which to thank society.

Shakespeare must have loved every minute of it and it is my opinion that this is where his theatrical experience was gained. In all probability, he was given an apprenticeship and, from such humble beginnings, he was able to see what he wanted to do in life. I am sure he corrected scripts and slowly added his own ideas. Then, finally, he discovered the gift of transcribing from classical plays of the period and preparing them for the stage.

This is where Shakespeare's streak of genius shows through; not in the sonnets and soliloquys which people rave about, but in his ability to adapt dramatic extracts from historical and classic plays for the theatre. So, I have a simple answer to the question of the lost years. He just became a strolling player himself until, probably aged about 18, he arrived, well versed in the theatrical arts of both writing and acting, ready to set the London stage alight.

Sometimes, the right answers are the simple ones.

But, what do we know about his early years in London? Aubrey, the historian, relates that he "did act exceedingly well" and "began early to make essays at dramatic poetry, which at that time was very low, and his plays took well". Aubrey says Shakespeare was "about 18" at the time.

It was not unusual in the late 16th and early 17th centuries for young men to seek their fortunes in London. For instance, another youth fron Stratford, John Sadler, born in 1586, set out alone to escape a marriage and "joined himself to a carrier (on a good horse supplied by friends) and came to London", according to tradition. He sold the horse in Smithfield, but not having any acquaintances in the city, went from street to street asking if anyone wanted an apprentice.

Eventually, a Mr Brooksbank, a grocer, gave him a job. Some years later, John Sadler was one of the wealthiest grocers in London and when he died he left a large estate, including property in Virginia, America.

Thomas Betterton, the actor and Nicholas Rowe, Shakespeare's first biographer, both related the story that

William's first employment at the London playhouses was to take care of the gentlemen's horses who came to enjoy the plays. There were only two theatres regularly open in London when William arrived - The Curtain and The Theatre - both beyond the city walls in open fields. The best way to reach them was by horseback.

Rowe went on to state that William was eventually "received into the company (of the playhouse) then in being at first in a very mean rank". Another report says he began as a prompter's attendant. At least seven top companies were working in London under various patronages, including the Earls of Leicester, Worcester and Pembroke. Undoubtedly the best known was the Queen's company which was particularly active in touring the provinces. On the Queen's death, King James established The King's players and it was this company which Shakespeare joined.

Then began his most prolific period as he produced his masterpieces of intrigue and emotion. I have no doubt that he used his own experiences and those of his friends around him in shaping the plays and the Dark Lady and Fair Youth were lurking at the back of his mind when he put quill to paper.

Shakespeare's plays were as great an attraction at the royal palaces in the winter as in the open-air Globe theatre during the summer. At court, the pieces were known as "morals, stories, histories, comedies and antic plays" and the dramatist's company became the most popular contributors to the royal dramatic performances. It was a period of spectacular entertainment, sparkling wit, wild parties and romantic liaisons. And Shakespeare was at the centre of it all.

Meanwhile, back at home in Stratford, wife Anne coped with family life and three children, Susanna and twins Hamnet and Judith. Hamnet is widely recognised as Shakespeare's favourite and he was mortified in 1596 when the boy died aged 13.

Most reports say he stayed at court, writing his comedies and tragedies, until about 1610 when he retired to Stratford to live in the town's grandest house, New Place, but there is another suggestion, made in the middle of the last century, that he left in 1604, a year before the Gunpowder Plot. It may be something or nothing, but it is a fact that Francis Tresham and Robert Catesby, two of the plotters, were Shakespeare's cousins. And, no doubt, the plans were being laid in 1604 for Parliament to be blown up.

Did Shakespeare get wind of the scheme? Did he decide to move out of London before he was implicated? Was he asked for money to support the plot? Certainly, his parents were followers of the Catholic faith; John Shakespeare was fined for not attending Protestant church services. And, in "The Day Shakespeare Died", Hugh Ross Williamson wrote that Shakespeare received the last rites as a papist after lying in state at New Place for two days.

Yet, his remains are said to rest in Holy Trinity Church, Stratford.

J O Halliwell-Phillips pointed out that workmen in the 18th century were building a vault near to the grave of Shakespeare when part of the wall of the writer's vault collapsed. When they looked inside, there was no sign of a coffin.

If this is true, then this could be one of the greatest confidence tricks in history. I am unhappy about the fact that no word has been passed down about the funeral service. I made an attempt in 1973 to end the speculation about whether or not Shakespeare is buried at the church, but my request was turned down. I proposed that a hole be drilled in the floor of the chancel so that an endoscope with a camera attachment could be pushed down to inspect the vault.

Whatever the truth of the matter, if the tradition is correct and he was buried 17 feet below ground, it is doubtful if anything now remains as water from the nearby river Avon will have seeped through to wash away the evidence.

PART 2

CHAPTER 4

Find the lady

The final resting place of Mary Fitton was unknown, but I made it my business to find her. I needed to know more about her if I were to provide a convincing case about her claims as the Dark Lady, the type of woman who aroused feelings of both enchantment and despair.

After the court scandal and her banishment, there was a period of relative calm as Mary recuperated in the tranquility of her sister's home at Arbury. Yet, the two women must have discussed Mary's disgrace and, in examining this part of her life, I was hoping to turn up a document or letter recalling the event, with perhaps a reference, albeit veiled, to an association with William Shakespeare.

For instance, there is in existence a letter written by Mary to her sister in which there is a tantalising phrase reminiscent of the dramatist. The letter is at Warwick archives and it reads:

"To my dearest sister, Misstress Anne Newdigate. Since distance bears me from so great happiness as I can seldom hear from you, which when I do is so welcome as I esteem nothing more worthy and for love which I doubt not or shall be equalled with full measure, but least my lines too tedious were, and time that limits all things bears me of words which else could never cease to tell how dear you are, and with what zeal I desire your return, and can wish nothing in your hearts desire and will ever continue. Your affectionate Sister Mary Fitton".

The phrase "time that limits all things" has a familiar Shakespearean ring about it; was she unconsciously revealing her links with him in this letter?

Arbury provided a suitable retreat for Mary, but, as I mentioned earlier, she was soon involved in another affair, this time with a cousin and vice-admiral, Sir Richard Leveson. He was married to the daughter of the Lord High Admiral, which probably accounted for his rapid promotion in the Navy, but his wife was insane.

Much harassed by the situation, the vice-admiral installed Mary in his house at Perton Manor, near Wolverhampton, in the parish of Tettenhall. Mary lived there for two years and contemporary statements credited the couple with two illegitimate children, much to the distress of Mary's mother. The Tettenhall parish registers confirm the births.

The year of 1605 was an unfortunate one for Mary with the death of Sir Richard at the age of 36 and she was still suffering from this untimely blow when her father, Sir Edward, died the following year. In these circumstances, it was not surprising that she accepted an offer of marriage that same year from another naval officer, Captain William Polewheele, a friend of Sir Richard's. The captain moved in with Mary at Perton Manor.

The marriage lasted four years until Captain Polewheele died, leaving a son, William, a daughter who died in infancy, and a posthumous child whose advent was predicted in his will.

Mary remained free for three years, but, in 1612, she married John Lougher, Member of Parliament for Tenby, Pembrokeshire. This marriage lasted for 20 years of long-sought happiness. Two children ensued, Elizabeth and John, and Mary also became somewhat reconciled with her mother.

The next mention of John Lougher in the registers is of his death in 1635. The record of his burial is not at Tettenhall as one would expect, but I found a Bishop's transcript at Chester which confirmed "John Lougher, Gent of Perton, Staffordshire" was buried at Gawsworth on January 8, 1635.

The reason for this can only be guessed at. Perhaps Mary and John had gone to the family home for the celebrations of Christmas, 1634, and, while there, John had died and been buried at Gawsworth. Or, again, perhaps Mary had intended, on her death, to be buried at Gawsworth and, when her husband died, she decided to have his body transferred to the village to be buried near to her own eventual grave.

Mary lived on for seven years after John's death. Her will was made a year before she died and it was dated December 19,1640. I came across it after a lengthy search by Miss Alice Stanley, of the Probate Registry.

Previously, only the registrar's copy of the will had been asked for, and, to my knowledge, by only one person, a Mr Bridgeman, who was Lady Newdigate's research assistant, in the last century. The original was lodged in the archives of Somerset House and I was the first person to see it in 300 years.

It was probably her son, William, who wrote down the will for Mary because it begins "I, Mary Polewheele" and the Polewheele is crossed out and Lougher substituted. Various items are listed, one being a gift of £200 to Mary's grandchild Anne Gateacre out of £1,000 owed to her by her son-in-law Robert Charnock (the gentleman who married Mary's illegitimate daughter by Leveson, Ann Fitton). At the end of the will - which, oddly, was proved twice (in 1647 and 1653) - was her request to be buried at Gawsworth: "I bequeath my soul into the hands of Almighty God, my creator and redeemer, through whose merits, death and passion I hope to be one of his safe creatures and my body to be buried in the Parish Church or Churchyard at Gawsworth in Cheshire."

When Mary Fitton died on September 19, 1641 aged 63, she had outlived Shakespeare by 25 years. Even in death, she bequeathed a mystery to the world: No record of her burial is contained in the parish register at Gawsworth. This led me to believe that she must have been interred at Tettenhall where she died, but more shocks were in store - the archives of the diocese of Lichfield had been tampered with. Documentation from the year 1641 to 1653 had been destroyed.

Checking again at Gawsworth, I found the church register

for the years 1641 to 1655 and onwards intact, but I was informed that a Victorian curate in charge in 1851, a certain Reverend Massie, had burned "extra items and documents" relating to the period when Mary Fitton died. This was another instance in which information about Mary had been destroyed. In the church at Gawsworth, the third example awaited me. I knew I would find there the effigies of Mary and her family as part of the monument erected in memory of her father, Sir Edward. His effigy is lost, but the seated figure of his wife, Alice, and the kneeling figures of their four children survive.

The tomb was completed in 1629 and, according to 17th century records, the inscription on the wall near the monument read: "Here lieth Edward Fitton, son and heir of Sir Edward Fitton, Lord President of Connaugh and Treasurer of Ireland, who married Alice, ye daughter and only heir of John Holcroft Knight, who had by her four children, two sons and two daughters..." The last seven lines of the inscription had been obliterated; the same Reverend

Mary Fitton effigy
... at Gawsworth church

Massie, who burned the documents, had chiselled off the lines! What was Rev. Massie trying to hide?

The effigies of Mary Fitton and her sister, Anne, depicted black haired women. Mary's pansy crest was in evidence, on her collar. On all the existing portraits, she holds pansies in her hand or wears a tiny pansy crest on her cuff, sleeve or collar.

Gazing at the cold, stony face of Mary Fitton, I mused on the warm, passionate personality it failed to portray. I knew, in that instant, I would have to apply to open the family vault and find her coffin. Perhaps inside there would be an object bearing Mary's crest, or even a keepsake from Shakespeare himself.

But, before any such application, I had to be sure that she had not been buried anywhere else. So, off I went to Tettenhall, where she had died and, sure enough, there was a burial notice there. This was in complete contradiction to her last testament, but I was not too worried about that; at least I had found her final resting place. Or had I?

The parish church at Tettenhall was gutted by fire about 20 years ago and, despite an intensive search, I could not find Mary's grave. In three separate sources – Robert Plot's History of Staffordshire, Shaw's Staffordshire and the Reverend Jones' Tettenhall - each listed all graves, tombs, plaques and monuments, but there was no mention of Mary's body being at Tettenhall. Now we had a situation in which there was no grave and no record of her burial at her family's church.

Questions flooded into my mind. Had she been exhumed from Tettenhall and reburied at Gawsworth? Was she buried at an obscure church between Tettenhall and Gawsworth? At the time of Mary's death and her possible transportation to Gawsworth, the Civil War was brewing. There was the possibility that a party of people, including Mary's son and daughter, had made the long journey from Wolverhampton to Gawsworth to lay Mary in the family vault. Could they have run into trouble as the Civil War intensified? The Fittons were Royalist sympathisers and they may have had to abandon their task and bury their mother in a hurry in a churchyard on the way.

The Civil War could explain the mysterious fact that Mary's name was not entered in the Gawsworth parish register, because, at the onset of the war, Cromwell installed puritan vicars in place of Royalist rectors. He, knowing Mary Fitton's Catholic leanings, her Royalist inclinations, past escapades in Elizabeth's court and other scandalous associations, may have decided that a Christian burial was acceptable, but her name was not to be entered in the parish register.

It is well to remember that the Fittons were around at a

time of unrest and murder. Cromwell was intent on eradicating any connections with the old order. It became increasingly clear to me that the only way I was going to end all this speculation was to conduct a foot-slogging find-the-lady excercise along the route from Tettenhall to Gawsworth. I would have to visit every church on the way, rummage through every register and peer into every graveyard.

The trouble with grass is that it grows! And a lot of grass has shot up since Mary Fitton was alive, so there is little or no trace of graveyards which existed in her day. The first priority, then, was to get a 16th century map of the region and, thanks to the Staffordshire archives, I managed to obtain a photostat of such a map. With the help of the geography department of Leicester University, I was able to trace the road between Tettenhall and Gawsworth.

That done, I started the tedious but necessary search for Mary Fitton's grave. I began at Wolverhampton, went on to Brewood and, eventually, all the other churches and cemeteries along the route to Gawsworth. Nowhere did I find documents, or any other evidence that, during those distant years, a strange lady had been buried along the route. I looked at aerial surveys of the district, because old, forgotten burial places show up as lighter coloured patches on such photography. Again I drew a blank.

Then, I had a break. A friend asked me if I had ever been to Big Fenton Farm, near Congleton, as it was rumoured the grave in the garden there was that of the Dark Lady. I decided to investigate. Early one April morning, I set off from Kegworth, in Leicestershire, and my only thoughts were of the grave in the garden. Could this, at long last, be Mary Fitton's resting place? Nearing the small farms dotted around the countryside between the famous hill, the Cloud, and Congleton, it was not difficult to be caught up in the atmosphere of the district and let one's mind wander back to the days when the Fittons owned Gawsworth and the land about.

Their main farms were at Gawsworth, Buglawton and Fenton. The latter supposedly belonged to one of the uncles, Francis Fitton, who died in 1608, and is only three miles across the fields to Gawsworth Manor.

Where was the original road, and which direction did it take? The surprising answer presents itself when you enter the farmyard and stand before the front door of Big Fenton Farm. As the door opens, a road of cobblestones goes straight through the house! Looking out into the rear, I could see a grave in the garden, to the left.

The stone at the head of the grave was weather-beaten, so nothing could be deciphered on it, but I obtained permission from the farmer to excavate. With his help and that of one of his farm-hands, we dug down six feet and found a box. Inside were the remains of a dog! After such a tiring session with spade and shovel, this was frustration we could have done without; it was akin to unearthing a treasure chest, only to find rocks instead of rubies.

Yet, even in our moment of disappointment, there was compensation of a kind; scattered among the lumps of soil were pieces of putrified wood which had probably been part of a coffin. It made me wonder again whether Mary had been buried temporarily on the way to Gawsworth. Her uncle's farm would have been an ideal place to hide a corpse until the Civil War had waned. Mary's family could then have returned to dig her up and resume their grizzly journey to Gawsworth just down the road.

Whatever happened, one thing was sure - Mary was not in the grave at Fenton Farm today.

On the way back from Fenton, I was convinced more than ever that the logical solution was the right one; namely, that Mary WAS buried at Gawsworth, in accordance with her wishes. The elimination work had taken two years and been costly, but that was behind me now. It was back to Gawsworth, with all my thoughts concentrated on Mary Fitton's ancestral home.

In 1967, the then Ministry of Housing and Local Government gave me an aerial photograph of Gawsworth, taken at 10,000 feet during the survey for the M6 motorway. It showed extensive workings near the manor and also a clear indication that a secret tunnel had existed, leading from the west wing of the manor house to the crypt at St. James's Church - possibly the escape route for the priest and others during Cromwellian times.

The next step was an archaeological investigation at Gawsworth Manor, carried out by John Mansfield, of geology department at Leicester University, with an electron proton magnetometer. The purpose was to search for cellars or passageways under the lawns (the masonry walls of such cavities can give a magnetic anomaly, detectable with a magnetometer). Unfortunately, however, the investigation proved fruitless.

Next, through the assistance of Professor Chadwick of Loughborough University, I contacted the Army at Stafford where Major John Howard, Commander of the 30th Brigade of Royal Engineers, promised that he would provide equipment and men to help the research.

With the Royal Engineers, I went to Gawsworth Manor in June, 1967 and made 18 trial holes, some of them 25 feet deep, to find out what was beneath. We used electronic apparatus, echo-sounding instruments and the like, apart from taking examples of the sub-soil. There was no sign of any burial and neither did we come upon any secret subterranean passages.

Undaunted, it was at this stage that I decided more dramatic measures were needed. I wrote to the rector of Gawsworth church and made a formal application to open the Fitton vault, should I find it, pledging assurance that a recognised academic body would sponsor my work.

The vault was the obvious place to look for Mary Fitton's coffin, but the entrance to the vault was unknown. The Fitton tomb was originally placed, together with the effigy of Sir Edward, close to the east wall of the church. Subsequently, the group of figures depicting Dame Alice and her children was moved westwards and set up against the north wall. A fillet of stone was inserted to fill the gap where the moulding of the tomb slab left a cavity in the wall.

The rector of Gawsworth suggested that I should conduct a preliminary investigation at first, to save a lot of money, hard work and possible further disappointment. In consequence, with Major Howard and his men, I made preliminary investigations lasting four months to try to find the entrance to the vault. We bored exploratory holes, made many probes and echo soundings, and in the end decided that the lost entrance lay somewhere close to the monuments on the north side of the chancel.

On February 24,1969, four years after I set out on my foot-slogging quest to solve the Dark Lady riddle, we excavated a hole to a depth of six feet. There was nothing. After numerous metal probes, it looked as though we were out of luck again. The entrance did not seem to exist. Then, quite suddenly, rough brickwork was uncovered on the right, facing the northern nave direction. Feverishly, we cleared away the sand; the brickwork was irregular and rough. Was this the lost entrance?

We pressed on. Captain Preece and an assistant carefully penetrated the brickwork and underneath we found a much smoother wall. This, in turn, was pierced and, to my delight, an entrance was found into what appeared to be the family vault of the Fittons! On entering, I was filled with despair. There were no coffins, no jewellery, no family mementoes, not even the nameplates from the coffins - just a heap of skeletal remains. It was a shocking mess and it looked as though grave-robbers had been at work.

Such was our dismay that we did not realise immediately this was uncharacteristic of grave-robbers. They would have been after jewellery and other other valuables; they would not have been concerned with the coffins or bodies. Yet it was apparent that efforts had been made to destroy everything.

As we explored, we came across a significant find. A small trenching shovel lay among the rotting wood and human remains, and it had been cast in the middle of the last century. According to experts at Leicester Museum, such tools were used by the artillery in the Crimean War. Here was proof that, not only 17th century grave-robbers or Commonwealth troops had been in the vault, but also Victorians.

Major Howard analysed the findings. He stressed that all the remains were in an area of approximately six feet six inches by five feet six inches. This section of the floor was covered in a layer of lime to a depth of two inches - an obvious attempt to destroy the bodies. In addition to bones and fragments of wood, several large lumps of congealed material were present. One of the doctors present suggested that they might be the mummified contents of the intestines of the bodies.

Beneath the skeletons, two courses of brickwork were removed from the floor, indicating a comparatively recent entry, with the lime having had time to destroy a lot of material, but not long enough to burn all the bones. In his analysis, Major Howard also emphasised that many of the joints in the brickwork had been roughly re-pointed. The texture of the cement was not much more than 100 years old and it corresponded to the mortar used in bricking up the end of the vault.

The dating of the material made it not only possible but highly probable that the recent destruction was carried out in 1851 when Reverend Massey burned documents and chiselled off inscriptions. So, instead of answers to the Dark Lady dilemma, I was left with more questions:

Fitton family vault remains

... a pathologist examines remains from the Fitton family vault at Gawsworth

Why open a vault already thoroughly plundered by grave-robbers?

Why try to destroy bodies which were possibly embalmed?

Why try to camouflage the entrance?

Why was there no written evidence of this re-opening of the Fitton vault?

In the last century, careful records were kept of all major and even minor building work conducted in or around the church, but, as we know, a certain Victorian curate burned some "extra items and documents" in 1851. Did these documents refer to the re-opening of the vault? It is ironical that the lime did not destroy all the bones in the tomb. The pathologists of Stoke-on-Trent General Hospital found that a single left tibia and a fibula belonging to an older male showed traces of syphilitic periostisis and it was considered that this was tertiary acquired syphilis rather than the congenital form of the disease (incidentally, it was the earliest syphilitic bone found in Britain).

Pathologists later made rough guesses about the ages of the individuals in the vault. None of the remains belonged to a 63-year-old woman, the age at which Mary Fitton died. However, the ages DID match up with those of Sir Edward Fitton, Mary's father, of Alice Fitton, and also of their son, Edward Jr., and his wife. So, I had still not found Mary Fitton's burial place. But I had found enough to sustain my determination to push on.

Once the pathologists had completed their report on the Fittons' remains, the bones were put back in the vault and it was re-sealed. A burial service was also conducted by the rector of Gawsworth. I returned home to reflect on the operation so far and I scrutinised the photographs taken at the time of the dig. It was not long before I began to have doubts that we had found the Fitton vault after all!

The photographs and the measurements of the area in which the bodies lay seemed to suggest a different answer - that what we had stumbled upon was, in fact, a passageway and not a vault at all. The burial chambers were probably elsewhere, leading off the passage. I noticed on one of the photographs another opening on the left side. The opening seemed to lead into a second chamber. Perhaps the bodies of John Lougher and Mary were there?

But what of the other bodies in the passageway? It was apparent that in the Commonwealth period the family vault of Sir Edward Fitton had been robbed and the remains had been tipped out of their coffins into the main passage leading from the vault. The coffins and non-precious metals must have been thrown back into the burial chamber, leaving just the remains of Sir Edward and his family scattered over the floor of the passage. That was the sight which met my gaze when we first opened what was thought to be the Fittons' family vault.

So, I made arrangements for another trek to Gawsworth

to explore the area around the passage and, in August, 1970, we set to work on the south side of the chancel with a drill loaned by Newcastle University geology department. After three probes produced no results, we moved the heavy equipment towards the altar. Here the drill suddenly slipped and the machine almost went through the floor. We had certainly found a cavity of some sort.

Out came the endoscope and I poked it down the hole. Below was a crypt which no-one knew existed, and adjacent was a vault containing three coffins. Above the vault stood the effigy of Francis Fitton, so logic dictated that this crypt was that of Francis, Mary's favourite uncle. He stood by her when her relationships with other members of the family were strained and, since it was known that Francis Fitton's wife was buried in Westminster Abbey, it was reasonable to suppose that the other two coffins were those of Mary Fitton and her last husband, John Lougher.

It took two more days of drilling before we could photograph the coffins, or at least the parts of the coffins visible through the holes. One still retained some of its leather covering bearing a crest in the shape of a skull with wings. Earlier, in the church, I had noticed on the wall an heraldic shield with a similar crest (skull and bat's wings); this was most probably the insignia of Francis Fitton.

Mary Fitton's coffin
... the coffin which Arthur Marlowe believes contains the shrouded remains of Mary Fitton

One of the other coffins had copper rivets around its edges (the green copper oxide showed up under the endoscope light). It was difficult to go any farther without a camera, so I asked for one and it was attached to the end of the endoscope. We had a few attempts before we were successful in taking a picture of the shrouded head of a corpse and part of the coffin. It was the first time this photographic technique had been used and I would certainly recommend it as a valuable aid to archaeology.

Thus ended our preliminary investigation. We had discovered a crypt, an annexe, three coffins and what might have been a dispatch box. The only way of finding out whether Mary Fitton was in the annexe was to open it.

But, first, I had to seek permission to open the crypt. I made a detailed formal application, pointing out Mary Fitton stated in her will that she wished to be buried at Gawsworth, and that, after eliminating other possible burial sites, I had found a vault containing a coffin which might be hers. The endoscope photographs provided additional evidence.

Nevertheless, when the application arrived at the office of the Bishop of Stockport, he opposed it. I tried in vain to have the decision reconsidered, so I appealed against the ruling and a consistory court was convened on May 10, 1971. Although I think my appeal was put forward capably, dealing with any possible objections in canon law, the Lord Chancellor upheld the bishop's decision - there was insufficient evidence to justify taking such a drastic step as opening the crypt.

This was an unexpected set-back. Unexpected because, earlier, I had been permitted to find, excavate and study the contents of the passageway in which the remains of members of the Fitton family had been found. With the help of the Army, pathologists and forensic scientists, I had accomplished that project without a single complaint. Yet, further excavation which might lead to important discoveries was refused, even though I had more evidence than at the time of my first request.

I could be accused of being biased, but I think it worth recording that BBC television interviewed an expert in canon law and he expressed the opinion that there was no adequate reason for rejecting my application. I was forced to consider the possibility that influential quarters were making sure I did not continue with my search. As I have shown, factions in the last century covered up historical events concerning Mary Fitton. Was it still going on?

The Parochial Church Council had given permission, the rector had given permission, the bishop of the local diocese had given permission and the diocesan advisory council had given permission. Yet, out of the blue, an objection from outside the area had been lodged. How did the suffragan bishop know? Had he been tipped off, and instructed that the dig must be stopped?

Despite the objection, I was still confident the court would rule in my favour, but the Chancellor of the Diocese of Chester said that to interfere with the coffin, as I was suggesting, would require a separate application. "I feel strongly that, unless there is some very good reason, whether in the cause of history or literary knowledge or what is commonly known as a public utility, the dead should be allowed to rest."

He rejected the application with regret, but felt the chances of a useful discovery were remote. I left the church bitterly disappointed, but I was determined to try again.

Ten months later, in March, 1972, I was allowed to return to Gawsworth to re-examine the contents of the annexe through the endoscope. I was accompanied by the Loughborough University photographic unit. I studied the coffin with the rivets on it. Near the coffin was a ring of metal still attached to a piece of wood which had fallen from the lid. The ring looked like a door knocker and there was a design on it. Although I had my own ideas about the design, I was reluctant to say anything until other members of the team had had a look. There was little doubt; there was general agreement it was a flower. And the flower appeared to be a pansy. My assistant sketched the crest in a notebook and the photographer took his picture.

Now, although the church authorities had attempted to thwart me, I was convinced I had found the vault of Mary Fitton.

I have thought many times about those heady days of 30 years ago and, although my research has taken me to many other places since, it has always been my ambition to return to Gawsworth and persuade the powers-that-be, "in the cause of history" and "literary knowledge", that I be allowed to open the flower-crested coffin. Who knows what is inside?

I asked a pyschologist if a woman who had received amorous poems from an admirer in the past would destroy them when she married to avoid detection. I wanted to know if the Dark Lady might have retained the sonnets, which were such poems. The pyschologist said that, even if the poetry were uncomplimentary (e.g. "the bay where all men ride"), she would keep them - to inflate her ego.

His answer confirmed my view that the Dark Lady (Mary Fitton?) could have taken poems dedicated to her by Shakespeare to her tomb. An instruction, not necessarily in the will, may have stated that "valuable papers for no-one's eyes but mine" should be placed in a despatch box or in her coffin. Manuscripts have been found in readable condition after centuries away from light. So, if the coffins I saw have not been tampered with, the possibility exists of sonnets waiting to be discovered at Gawsworth.

There could be other finds. For instance, in Shakespeare's day, Nicholas Hilliard produced ink portraits of prominent people as keepsakes. They were contained within lockets with clasped fronts which snapped tight to preserve the ink. In one of the pictures at Arbury Hall, Mary Fitton is wearing a Hilliard. Is it in her coffin? Does it contain a picture of Shakespeare?

CHAPTER 5

The Tresham puzzle

Earlier, I briefly touched on the Gunpowder Plot and Francis Tresham, who was a member of a family headed by Sir Thomas Tresham.

Sir Thomas' wife, Muriel, was a Throckmorton before marriage. The Throckmortons came from Coughton, in Warwickshire, and were related to the prominent Arden family, also of Warwickshire. This is where the link with Shakespeare is established, for William's mother, Mary, was the daughter of Robert Arden, a rich farmer. Sir Thomas Tresham, like most Catholics in those days, suffered for his beliefs, spending years in prison and under house arrest. His son, Francis, married Anne Tufton, daughter of Sir John Tufton, from Hothfield, in Kent, and they produced two daughters, Lucy and Elizabeth. A son, Thomas, died in infancy.

In his youth, Francis was regarded as something of a tearaway, easily led astray, with a scant appreciation of the value of money. Alongwith the earls of Essex and Southampton, he was involved in a plan to assassinate Queen Elizabeth a year or so before her death. My interest in him was alerted when I learned that he escaped a sentence of death for his part in the escapade. His punishment was a fine, albeit a heavy one.

Essex duly went to the block, although Southhampton, no doubt helped by his position as a privy counsellor - and a personal plea by his mother to the Queen - was spared. But why would Tresham have been saved?

Perhaps Lord Salisbury, Robert Cecil, saw the opportunity

of using him at a later date as a secret agent. Cecil was obsessed with Catholics; he saw them under every bed and believed there would be no peace in England until the country was rid of them.

He launched a campaign to eliminate as many powerful Catholics as possible, figuring that, once the landed gentry of the faith had been disposed of, the country's troubles would be over.

Tresham's cousin, Robert Catesby, leader of the Gunpowder Plot, lived in a beautiful manor house at Ashby St Legers, in Warwickshire. At the entrance, there is a fine, timbered structure aptly called the Gate House, where, according to popular belief, the Gunpowder Plot was hatched.

When the plot was uncovered, Catesby tried to escape, but was shot by the sheriff's men, later decapitated and buried in an unknown grave.

One of the other plotters, Sir Edward Digby, is an interesting character. He could have met Shakespeare by introduction through either Catesby or Tresham. He came from a village in Leicestershire called Stoke Dry, where his parents were buried, and lived at the local manor house until his adventures in London came to light.

Stoke Dry's church contains a room over the north door where, it is said, the plot was discussed. I carried out a drilling at the church to try to find what lay beneath the floor, but there was no sign of a vault. This is not surprising, for I later read the church architect's report of 1896 which stated that a number of faults had been located in the building and, as a result, certain sections of the floor had been raised.

The architect said the chancel needed special attention and added: "Should any burial places be found, these should be filled in with cement."

I do not intend to dwell unduly on the Gunpowder Plot, but the accepted view that young Tresham died in the Tower of London after he and his accomplices were caught may be a fabrication. The oft related story is that his severed head was put on public view on a stake outside Northampton Castle, yet Fr. Francis Edwards reports in his "Guy Fawkes, or the

Real Story of the Gunpowder Plot?" that Robert Cecil devised a plan which allowed him to escape to France.

To placate the church and court, he prepared a statement declaring that Tresham had been executed, but he had been in the Tower only a month when the keeper, a man called Waad, was told his prisoner was to be freed.

Tresham's wife, Anne, was allowed to slip into the Tower at the change of guard posing as a servant. Two "servants" were seen to leave and the guards later reported that one seemed to be distraught; the distraught "servant" was Tresham, covered in a hooded cloak brought in a basket by Anne.

A boat had been laid on for Tresham who melted away into the night towards the south coast and freedom. There are reports that Tresham moved on from France to Spain and Italy, but I am convinced that, eventually, the pull of home would have tugged at Tresham's heart. In 1610, four years before his mother's death, he was still abroad, it seems.

In that year, Robert Pearson wrote a letter to a Jesuit priest from Rome. It said: "I have not written to your Reverence since I replied to the compliments sent to me by Mr. Tresham. I do not doubt that your Reverence will gather from my reply the difficulties that we have had to put up with from needy people in this long exile of theirs. It frequently happens that these who have received most help, favours and benefits from us, over many years, suddenly begin to complain when at last they fail to get all the satisfaction they demand."

If Francis Tresham had returned to England, where would he have been buried? And would he have brought back any letters or documents revealing an earlier association with Shakespeare?

Working on the theory that, if you find the woman, the man will be close by, I concentrated my efforts on searching for Anne, his wife. My investigations began at Rushton Hall, in Northamptonshire, the former home of the Treshams and now a school for blind children. I was helped enormously by the Department of the Environment, the Royal Institute of the Blind and the headmaster, Mr Robert Orr. The purpose was to locate the vault of the Treshams where, it was hoped, Anne and Francis would be found.

Sir Thomas Tresham died in September, 1605, only two months before his son's notorious role in the Gunpowder Plot, and he was buried beneath the chancel of the old St. Peter's Church at Rushton. His wife, Muriel, died a few years later and was, reputedly, buried by his side.

Long after the death of Sir Thomas and his wife, St Peter's Church fell into disuse and the then owner of the hall, Viscount Cullen, successfully applied for a faculty for its removal to enhance the view of the hall. As a result, the church disappeared.

Over the years, the ground around the site of the church was landscaped and lowered at least three feet. To find the foundations was a near impossibility for one man alone, so I called in the Royal Air Force. They took a series of photographs of the hall and grounds to see if the outline of the foundations would show up.

In 1979, the original plan of the forecourt of the hall was accidently found in a court book at Delapre Abbey, the Northamptonshire Record Office, and it was a combination of this and the aerial photographs which helped to firmly establish the position of the old church.

The plan had been drawn up in 1736 for Lord Cullen when he made his application to the Diocesan Registrar at Peterborough for the faculty.

The task of working out the exact position of the church was undertaken by some of my friends who worked long hours with their surveying equipment and marked out the outer and inner walls of the church and its tower.

Despite all this, we were unable to find the Tresham vault. We came to the conclusion the ground had been lowered so much during the landscaping that the arched roof of the vault - which would have stood proud - had been demolished and filled in for safety reasons. However, we do know that four coffins were found there at one time and I am of the opinion that the first two were probably Sir Thomas, Knight Templar and his wife, and the other two, Sir Thomas Tresham and his wife, Muriel, parents of Francis.

Ever optimistic, I resolved to try another angle. In the late

16th century, Sir Thomas ordered the construction of the famous Roman Bath of Rushton Hall. Did his favourite piece of architecture hold a secret for us to unravel?

The bath was fed from the nearby St Peter's Spring and, soon after starting investigations, we uncovered a pipe which carried the water from the spring to the bath. To reach it, I climbed and fought my way through a jungle of undergrowth. Almost hidden by old trees, ivy and moss, I came upon a section of stoneworks. It was the Roman Bath. Although delapidated through age, it was readily identifiable, matching its description in "Northamptonshire Notes and Queries." Within the walls were niches which had once contained statues of goddesses of mythology. There were also two tablets bearing inscriptions.

What a place of beauty it must have been in the days of Sir Thomas. At any minute, I fully expected to see the colourful costumes of the gentry making their way through the glade towards the bath.

A statement in "Northamptonshire Notes and Queries" claimed that a vault had been discovered near to the bath in the late 18th century. This was a mystery. Why build a vault such a distance from the church? Could it have been consecrated ground? Was this the vault in which Francis had been interred or was it used as a hiding place after he came back from overseas?

The "Northamptonshire Notes and Queries" stated that in the 1840s, during remodelling of the grounds, there were a quantity of fragments dug up around the vicinity of the bath, Faith, Hope and Charity figures that probably, at one time, decorated a formal garden.

Intrigued by the prospect of finding a vault, we set to work with tractor and auger, making a number of holes to a considerable depth. Again, there was no brickwork of any kind, or even a cavity. It seemed to me that, if there had been a vault within the vicinity of the bath, then we would have come across something to indicate its whereabouts. The answer, regrettably, appeared to be that it had been demolished and filled in.

During the Second World War, the Army used the area extensively and half-track vehicles constantly moved to and fro across the land. They could have crushed the top of a vault and, for safety's sake, the soldiers probably filled it in with rubble.

So, what next? For 200 years or more, it has been suggested that a subterranean passage links Rushton Hall with the well known Triangular Lodge and many a countryside tale has grown up around it. Our next task, then, was to find the tunnel and we focussed our attention on the lodge, a folly built by Sir Thomas in 1593.

We investigated the entire building. On the top floor, there was a priest hole behind the fireplace, but there was nothing of consequence on any of the other floors. Next, we decided to excavate the cellar. Normally, when searching for a tunnel, people dig down to a depth of about four feet until reaching the ironstone bed without finding anything. Then they give up. Our approach was different. We dug down the side of the foundations in three corners. Mr John Thompson, a civil engineer, came across the first course of bricks at four feet and a rough course of lime mortar. Below this, he discovered the foundations made of extraordinary brickwork.

Below ground there was no indication of a keystone arch, or, alternatively, a lintel construction. It would seem correct to assume that, if a step system had led to a tunnel entrance, the side walls would have continued for a considerable depth of, say, some five feet, but this was not so.

In order to conceal a step system and tunnel entrance, one would have expected to find a slab or trap door arrangement. A stone slab with a ring pull, which could equal the floor area below stairs, would be far too heavy for a person to lift. Also there did not appear to be any lip arrangement built into the horizontal courses to suggest that there was ever any support for a slab or trap door.

From the initial inspection, it seemed the loading imposed by the mass of blockwork in the wall was adequately balanced by the ground bearing pressure that one might expect at the depth below the untrimmed stones. The fact that the building was standing bore witness to this. What is more important, without some form of underpinning at the stairwell corner of the building, it might have collapsed by now if there had been a crude tunnel.

So, there we have it. Definitely, no indication of a tunnel to the Triangular Lodge.

We moved on to Rushton Hall itself. If nothing existed at the Triangular Lodge, there was a possibility that a tunnel might be found there. Before starting, the RAF helped out once again, carrying out an aerial survey from Rushton village and over the hall in the direction of the Triangular Lodge, this time using an infra-red scanning device. The results were extremely unusual. At first glance, the photographs seemed a little disappointing, until certain details were noticed, indicating there might be some form of entrance or tunnel.

We began by investigating the cellars which went down to a depth of about 12 feet, with foundations of about six feet. The cellars were extensive, taking up most of one side of the quadrangular-shaped hall. Off one of the cellars was a long corridor which contained what appeared to be a foundation wall made of blocks of ironstone. It looked formidable. While giving thought to the situation, it suddenly dawned on me that I was utterly wrong in my assumption. It was not a foundation wall at all, for, on returning to the cellar, I saw the foundation wall there in front of me. This was a quandary which needed clearing up.

We set about drilling two holes in the ironstone wall and, after about 90 minutes, much to the surprise of everyone, we broke through into a cavity. Another hole was then drilled at the same level and angle with a bigger drill, through which the six feet long endoscope was pushed, while the light source went through one of the smaller holes.

To say that we were all astonished at what we saw would be putting it mildly. There, through the endoscope was what looked like a magnificent, ironstone arched tunnel. At the far end - the north end - it appeared there had been a fall of rock or soil. Suffice to say, we had seen enough to whet our appetites but we had to wait a week - a week full of suspense and anticipation at what we might find - before permission was given to break into the tunnel.

It was a Sunday morning in October, 1979, when we started the work of taking away the first skim of bricks with the help of an electric kango hammer. Behind the bricks was an ironstone wall, which we knocked down with some difficulty. Then we came across yet another wall, in which we made a hole just big enough for a man to wriggle through. First, we turned on the examination lamps. What a wonderful sight it was, the lovely, dressed ironstone arch standing out proudly, having withstood the passing of centuries without any real sign of age.

We were probably the first to gaze upon it in 250 years. It was beyond comprehension and so exciting. The sight struck us so forcibly that all we could do was to look at each other in utter silence. We had found, so we thought, an early 16th century tunnel. Its length was 27 feet and, at the north end, the wall bricks and stone floor ran into soft earth. There the "tunnel" stopped.

But we soon discovered it was not the mystery tunnel after all. It was, in fact, an enlarged priest's hide, four feet high and about the same in width. Anyone hiding there would have had to remain doubled up in a cramped position - most uncomfortable. But we saw that someone had used it and, without doubt, it was a priest.

A search revealed three clay pipes of about five inches in length, with thick stems and small bowls. There were also pieces of a carved wooden stool, some oyster shells and a large iron poker. There was also a broken glass wine flagon, identified as late 17th century, as well as part of a 16th century Cardinal Balinmar jug which we found buried in the earth floor. And, also in the earth, we came across a footprint! We promptly recorded it with a camera.

Pieces of stained glass and meat bones were discovered, also indicating someone had spent some time there.

The most important find was in the middle of the hide - a priest's Communion bell. Most of these articles were later put on display in Rushton Hall.

Shortly after it was found, the bell was stolen, but it re-appeared through the mail; obviously the thief's conscience gained the better of him, or her.

The conclusion I came to was that the hide had been used by Fr. Campion (SJ) and Fr. Parsons (SJ), who were successfully hidden from the agents of Salisbury and Topcliffe. Under torture, however, Fr. Campion confessed that Sir Thomas had hidden him at Rushton Hall. Tresham, of course, denied this. He was asked to swear an oath but refused, saying he could never use a Protestant Bible.

We can be reasonably certain that the priest's hide is of early 16th century origin. What more or less confirms this is the fact that the cellar, from where we made the holes into the hide, was constructed in the early part of the 18th century. That was apparent when we looked at the exterior of the building and compared it with the engraving of Winstanley and earlier architects' drawings. In other words, the cellar did not exist when the hide was in use.

When the 18th century building work was started, the labourers apparently came across the entrance to the hide. It was at this stage that the foundations of the new building were laid, thus covering the stone arch, which remained in-situ for more that 250 years until we uncovered it. The other end of the hide ends outside the west door of the hall. This presents a puzzle, for, when you look at where the stonework ends and the earth begins, it seems there has been a total collapse, suggesting there is a continuation of the cavity further along.

It is my assumption that this may well have been caused by the builders. On making a further inspection of the architect's drawing of the ground floor of the hall, I noted that, where the collapse had taken place, there was at one time a 16th century building, which must have been in need of considerable repair. When Sir William Cockayne took over the hall, he probably decided to demolish this particular part of the old building and infill a new portion.

It was probably at this stage that the workmen came across the hide and, seeing the large amount of ironstone bricks available, used them for the new foundations. That would explain why the hide ended and there was the absence of any stonework at the north end.

The earliest part of the building was erected by John Tresham, the builder, of Sywell, in 1498. This contained the library or state room which was extensively panelled. From the measurements of the hide, and its direction, it would seem that access to it was gained from this room by means of a short ladder.

The next place to investigate was the chapel, to try to find either a priest's hide or another means of access to the newly discovered hide which ended by the west door, below the chapel. This is quite a small room on the third floor and, because of its position, it can be assumed there was a quick getaway for an unfortunate priest who learned his enemies were near at hand. It was my belief that, if there were such a secret place, it would be between the outer and inner walls. The walls are three feet six inches thick - wide enough for a cavity to allow someone to hide, or even to escape downward and into the ironstone hide.

It was outside the west door, at the rear of the hall, that the exit from the hide would be located, possibly in an Italian-style garden which was a popular feature of such great houses. The exit or entrance could have been located under a plinth bearing a statue, or a sundial. The subterranean passage we found demonstrates the great care that Sir Thomas took to hide a priest, or anyone else. He had it constructed in such a manner that its presence had eluded searchers until we came across it.

Sitting quietly in the chapel, you sense the centuries roll back. Where the alter used to stand there is now a beautiful piece of stonework fixed to the wall by an oak beam. On the stonework is the Crucifixion of Christ, with Mary Magdalene and the people standing around him and also the two crosses of the thieves, bearing a Latin inscription. Sir Thomas had it placed there in 1577.

The hall held one other small surprise for us. It came when we were tapping the walls, hoping to find a secret panel. Behind an old wall was a cavity of about two feet by two and a half feet and, with the aid of the endoscope and lighting, we saw an old narrow, stone window frame in the style of the 16th century. Many years ago an extension was built on to this part of the hall. The window was blocked up and had been hidden from view for more than two centuries.

I thought I had come to the end of my archaeology at Rushton, but it is strange how something crops up out of the blue to send you off on another trail. Shortly after concluding my work at the hall, I read a report by the late Sir Gyles Isham, of Lamport Hall, Northamptonshire. Sir Gyles was responsible for bringing to light a considerable amount of background material about the Tresham family.

It was in one of his reports, entitled "Sir Thomas Tresham and his Buildings", that he made an unusual statement; I am sure he did not realise the importance of the last two words.

He was referring to the building of Triangular Lodge between 1595-1600 and he gave a clue to the mystery of the tunnel. Referring to the famous diary of his ancestor, Justin Isham, he stated: "When he visited Rushton, the year was 1668. He had dinner with Lord Cullen, and then discussed many things with some of the village folk afterwards.

"Among their discussions was this mythological tunnel leading from Rushton Hall to the Lodge."

Note the last two words "the Lodge." No mention of the "Triangular" Lodge which everyone aver the years had associated with the tunnel. This was a "Lodge in the Hawk Field at Rushton." I began to think very carefully about this "Lodge in the Hawk Field" and realised how important it could be.

I asked Mr David Paine, of Rushton Estates, whether he knew of a Hawk Field and he told me: ."There is no such name of a field in the papers and plans of the estate at this present day."

So, I went to Delapre Abbey, Northampton, the department of archives for the county, and asked to see their oldest tithe or enclosure maps. The earliest they had was a 1732 enclosure map of the entire Rushton Estate, which had been drawn up for Lord Cullen. There it was - Hawk Field Meadow, near to the old bridge which is part of the original Rushton Estate. The Hawk Lodge stood only a matter of 800 to 1,000 yards from the Triangular Lodge and practically in a direct line from north to south. To me, this was unusual.

Had everyone been wrong in the past in supposing the mysterious tunnel went to the Triangular Lodge, when really it went to Hawk Lodge?

I carefully examined an aerial photograph taken in 1968 by the RAF for Ordnance Survey. There, on the other side of the small bridge, were the giveaway white lines which indicated the outline of a small building. A closer examination revealed that what at first seemed to be the lines of a small structure took on the appearance of two buildings tightly butted together. It looked as though the Hawk Lodge foundations were twice the size of the Triangular Lodge.

Another look at the infra-red photographs taken by the RAF the previous year showed nothing to suggest a tunnel existed between that spot and the hall. However, the possibility could still not be ruled out that there might be a priest's hide, or a hiding place of some description. Some readers might think I am dwelling too long on the subject of a priest's hide. But the point cannot be emphasised too strongly that the period to which I am referring was one in which an escape route, or a hideaway, could be a matter of life or death. Today, this might sound melodramatic, but it was not the case during that part of our nation's history.

To be a Roman Catholic, especially one with influence, was most dangerous. To be a Roman Catholic priest was looked upon as treason and meant a sentence of death.

Another reason for investigating Hawk Lodge, in addition to finding the long-lost tunnel, was that a hide, containing objects such as those found in the hall cellars, might come to light. There was the chance that Francis Tresham had hidden something there. At that time, such objects might not have been of importance to him, but, today, any information or artefact of that age could be of immense value, particularly if it had any association with his cousin, William Shakespeare.

But the infra-red photographs, taken at 3,000 feet by the RAF from all points of the compass over the Rushton Estate, showed we had been wrong in our assumption about the Hawk Lodge location. On such photographs anything like stone, which is under the surface of the earth, is easily detectable. We could see the foundations of the Hawk Lodge quite clearly and the surprising thing was that they were not in the field known then as Hawk Field. This field stands on the far side of the bridge from the hall, on the other side of the River Ise, to the right. In fact, the foundations were on the hall side of the river and to the left of the bridge, in line with the old water mill site.

Apart from that, there was no sign of any tunnel, or even

anything resembling a cavity. After all the work undertaken on the estate, and all the aerial photographs, I think it can safely be said that no such secret tunnel or passage ever existed. The stories over the centuries of a subterranean escape route can be disregarded and put down to village folklore which, like many other stories and mysteries, is embellished with each generation.

My personal opinion is that the hide we found at the hall was discovered by the Cullen family. They would have had only candles to give them illumination in that confined space. Coming across the fall of earth they would imagine, as we did, that it continued on the other side. Like others, they would have heard the stories of the tunnel and would assume that this was it. Thus ended my work at Rushton Hall and its estate, although I am sure, in the coming years, others will still believe a tunnel exists between the hall and the lodge - Triangular or Hawk - and will spend endless hours on a hopeless quest.

William Shakespeare and Sir Thomas Tresham had much in common. They both expressed themselves in their respective ways. The difference between them was that Shakespeare put his feelings and thoughts into words, while Tresham indicated his faith by means of architecture.

Sir Thomas left us with a puzzle in the Triangular Lodge - a cryptagram en masse, a symbolic form of The Trinity. Without the aid of aerial photographs and accurate ordnance survey maps it would have been impossible to unravel the mystery, and the message, he left behind.

Let me explain. On one of the photographs, Rushton Hall can been seen at the apex of a triangle. The Triangular Lodge is on the left side, while the site of Hawk Lodge is on the right. What we have from the air, therefore, is an isosceles triangle. This man not only built things on a large scale, but left his religious mark on the landscape at Rushton, for the Triangular Lodge itself is also an isosceles triangle!

Immediately after the building was completed in August, 1596, having taken three years to erect, work commenced on Hawk Lodge. This proved to be a much easier task than the Triangular Lodge, for it was finished by the end of the following year.

Miss Finch, in her book on the Tresham family, said: "The Lodge, the Hawk Lodge, could have been ornamental". Even if it were ornamental, and we have no reason to believe otherwise, it probably was not on the same grand scale as the Triangular Lodge, for Hawk Lodge took less than 18 months to finish. What did Hawk Lodge look like?

The aerial photographs show the symmetrical pattern of the old foundations and you get the feeling that you are looking at a half circle. If you draw this circle, and than add another to make it even, you have a lodge something similar to the Globe Theatre. So, we have a triangle which could mean Alpha, the Beginning, and then the complete circle of the Hawk Lodge giving almost the shape of Omega, the End. Alpha and Omega, the Beginning and the End.

To quote from Revelations, chapter 1, verse 8: "I am Alpha and Omega, the beginning and the ending, saith the Lord, which is, and which was, and which is to come, the Almighty". Although this can be seen only from above, Sir Thomas Treshan no doubt worked it all out on paper so that everything would be perfect and the message, once realised, would be understood.

CHAPTER 6

Elizabeth found

To be honest, during the past 150 years, few of the mysteries surrounding Shakespeare have been unravelled. So, you can well imagine the great feeling of satisfaction experienced by myself and my team of enthusiastic helpers when we solved one which had baffled historians since the middle of the 19th century.

Although many women influenced Shakespeare's life and his works, there was one who was especially dear to his heart. This was his only grandchild, Elizabeth, who was born at Stratford in 1608. She was the only child of Shakespeare's elder daughter, Susanna.

The playwright saw his beloved grandchild reach the age of eight before he died. His will gives a clue to his feelings for Elizabeth, for in it he bequeathed her his silver and £100 - a great deal of money in those days. Also, she was to inherit all his property and effects at Stratford after her mother's death. Historian Halliwell-Phillipps said that perhaps Elizabeth's greatest attribute, inherited from her grandfather, was her business acumen. She knew what she wanted and how to get it, for she gained wealth, land and a manor house.

In many ways, Elizabeth reminds me of Mary Fitton. Mary, although a courtesan, 10 years younger than Shakespeare, also had a goal in life, as well as a businesslike manner to help her reach the status she desired.

Elizabeth married Thomas Nash, of Stratford, a student at Lincolns Inn, in 1626 when she was then only 18 years old. The couple lived at New Place, which had belonged to her grandfather, and was left to her mother. They had been married for 20 years when Thomas Nash died at New Place on April 4,1647, leaving Elizabeth alone; there were no children.

Despite this setback, Elizabeth was well provided for in worldly goods. She had a substantial dowry from her husband; she had inherited half her father's property, and would succeed to the rest, as well as to the property left by Shakespeare to his elder daughter, Susanna, on her mother's death. However, she was not destined to remain a widow for long, for John Bernard, Lord of the Manor of Abington, Northampton, came into her life. It is possible that the two had known each other for some time, even before the death of John Bernard's first wife - also an Elizabeth - for it is said that he, too, owned property in Stratford.

His first wife died in March, 1642 while in her early 30s and was laid to rest in the family vault in the Church of St. Peter and St Paul, Abington, on March 30. She had had eight children, although three of them, two sons and a daughter, pre-deceased their mother.

Two years after her death, the remains of another son were carried into the family vault - all this during the Civil War in which John Bernard does not appear to have taken an active part (at the early age of six, he became the head of the Bernard family on the death of his father, Baldwin Bernard, and was made a ward of the king). That left four children of John's first marriage still alive - three daughters and a son. Mary, the second daughter, was the first to marry. She gave her hand to Thomas Higgs, of Colesbourne, Gloucestershire, on July 7,1657.

Elizabeth, the eldest daughter, became the wife of Henry Gilbert, of Locko, Derbyshire, on February 15,1657-8, while Eleanor, the third daughter, married Samuel Cotton, of Hinwick, Bedfordshire, on September 8,1659. Unfortunately, the surviving son, Charles, who was John Bernard's only hope of succession in the male line, died in May, 1651, aged 11. He was called Charles after an earlier son who had also died.

John Bernard and Elizabeth Nash were married at Billesley, near Stratford, on June 5,1649, only a few months after the execution of King Charles 1. The bride was then 41 and her bridegroom three years her senior.

A month after the marriage, Susanna Hall, Shakespeare's daughter, died and Elizabeth became the owner of New Place, along with other properties. However, it is not known how often she visited the house - or that of her late father, which she had also inherited - after her second marriage, which, like her first, proved childless.

The Bernard family were well known in Northamptonshire for they had held Abington Manor for more than 200 years. John Bernard came to the notice of King Charles 11 on or about November 25,1661, and shortly after his accession, Charles made him a baronet, although it was usual to describe him as a knight. As a result of the titled order bestowed on her husband, Elizabeth Bernard now became Lady Elizabeth Bernard, Lady of the Manor of Abington.

Regrettably, I have not been able to find any written evidence which would reveal details of Sir John Bernard's social life, his character, or even his political leanings, but I suspect he was a staunch royalist awaiting the day when the monarchy would be restored. I have tried to find more about Sir John through his father, Baldwin (who also married twice), but to no avail. What we do know is that he was a wealthy man, for, not only did he own the manor, but also a vast estate.

Lady Elizabeth died in February, 1670, at the age of 62, and, as far as it was known, her remains were placed in what was then the family fault at the east end of the south aisle of the Church of St Peter and St. Paul on the Abington estate.

What is strange, however, is that, although I believe Sir John had been extremely fond of his second wife, no memorial was raised in the church to her memory. However, some time between 1900 and 1904 her name was inscribed on Sir John's memorial slab in the floor on the south aisle.

A translation of the Latin inscription on the slab reads:

"Here lies the remains of the most noble
man, John Bernard, Soldier, famous because
of this father, grandfather, great-grandfather

and other ancestors, Lord of the
Town of Abington for 200 years and more.
He died in the 69th year of his age on
the 3rd March in the 1673rd year
since the Blessed Mary gave birth."

Then, added below this, in plain English lettering: "Also to Elizabeth, second wife of Sir John Bernard, Kn. (Shakespeare's granddaughter and the last of the direct descendants of the poet) who departed this life on the 17th February, 1670, aged 64 years."

Note the difference about Elizabeth's age.

The inscription gives it as 64, but, if she were born in 1608, she would have been 62 on her death, as stated previously.

According to Mrs Napier's "The Bernards of Abington," Sir John sold The Manor, Lordship and Advowson of Abington, with Court Leet, Court Baron and Fishery in the River Nen from Northampton meadow to Weston meadow, to William Thursby, of the Middle Temple, London, esquire, for 13,750L" on December 4 1669. That was 10 weeks before the death of Elizabeth and it seems one of the stipulations was that a survivor of the two should be allowed to live out the rest of their days in the old home.

In the parish register it states:

"Madam Elizabeth Bernard, wife of Sir John Bernard Knt., was buried 17th February, 1669." Here again, it will be noted the difference in dates between the parish register and the added inscription to her second husband's memorial slab. The latter states that she "departed this life on the 17th February, 1670". The register says that she was buried "17th February, 1669".

The day and month are irrelevent; it is the year which causes confusion. The reason is that, in those days, the parish register started the new year on March 25th, the month after Elizabeth's death. So, the church date is shown in the register as 1669, because 1670 did not start until the following month, even though it was the actual calendar year.

De Wilde states: "It is curious that this entry in the register is somewhat cramped and crowded upon a record of the burial of Thomas Hoe, labourer; it is the last in that year (the year then commenced on 25th March) and its appearance almost suggests an interpolation between the burial of Thomas Hoe and the heading of the coming year "Anno Domini 1670", as if the keeper of the register had written the heading that year, not expecting other burials.

"Of this last of the Shakespeares there is no other record. So far as it is known, no stone ever marked the place where she was buried."

He goes on to state: "Many comments have been made on this omission, and gloomy hints thrown out as to the domestic relations at Abington Manor. Malone observes that Sir John seems not to have been sensible of the honourable alliance he had made. Shakespeare's granddaughter would not, at this day, go to her grave without a memorial."

Of course, it must be remembered that the works of Shakespeare were not revered so much then as now. He had been dead for 54 years when Lady Bernard died - a period when, in all probability, his name and works were not widely known throughout Britain. Perhaps Sir John was averse to elaborate memorials. Not only does it seem he failed to erect one to Shakespeare's only grandchild, but it would also appear that he put up no memorial to his first wife, Elizabeth Edmondes, the mother of his children.

Mrs. Napier also points out: "Finally, it does not seem as if Lady Bernard herself greatly prized the traditions of her family. Her will which is witnessed by John Howes, Rector de Abington, and Francis Wickes, probably a servant, and begins 'In the name of God, Amen. I Dame Elizabeth Bernard' etc. etc. - testifies to her 'being in perfect memory (blessed be God), and mindful of mortality.'

"She then proceeds to give directions for the sale of her house in New Place, giving her 'loving cousin, Edward Nash, Esq., the first offer or refusal thereof, according to my promise formerly made to him'." Mrs Napier states that "in this will there is no hint of domestic dissensions; on the contrary, Lady Bernard showed a kindly feeling towards her husband's family."

To return to the lack evidence of a memorial to either of Sir John's two wives, it would seem it was a considerable time before the sepulchral monument was erected to the memory of his father. Baldwin died in 1610 aged 56 and it was not until 1636 that Sir John had the monument placed in the church, where it can be seen today, on the north wall of the chancel.

Mrs Napier wrote: "When John Bernard proceded to carry out his mother's last wishes as to her interment (she died in 1634), he doubtless awoke to the fact that no sepulchral honours had yet been made to his father, Baldwin, the Lord of the Manor.

"This is difficult to account for. Possibly some very simple slab or tablet had been deemed sufficient at the time, but did not satisfy his son, in the light of subsequent events, having regard also to the continued development of the taste for elaborate structure in memory of the dead.

"John Bernard now dedicated to his father a mural monument in alabaster, enriched by a shield with quarterings, and an inscription of some length, but not ostentatious, in which he names himself as the person who had carried out this filial duty." Sir John's death is certified by the rector, John Howes, who wrote: "Sir John Bernard, Knight, my noble and ever honoured patron, was buried 5th March, 1673/74."

The lack of reference to Lady Bernard until the turn of the 20th century, caused historians to doubt whether she was buried with her husband in the vault beneath the south aisle. This was the case until Halliwell-Phillipps' research. He said: "In the south aisle is an alabaster slab to the memory of John Bernard. Underneath this slab now is a vault belonging to the Thursby family who bought the Manor from John Bernard in 1669-1670, three months before his wife's death. The remains of John and Elizabeth are probably lost."

He gave no hint as to why he thought their remains were "lost," although other historians and researchers apparently accepted this view. But, I found it strange he should dismiss the subject so lightly. It was as if he could not be bothered to go any deeper to find out.

I felt something had to be done to either prove the remains were still there, or otherwise. If they were not in the vault, then at least it would confirm they had been moved so that the vault could be used by the Thursby family, the new owners of the manor after the Bernards. Thus, the decision was taken to carry out an investigation, and, with the permission of the rector, a preliminary probe was undertaken. A small hole was drilled in several places in the floor to find the exact location of the vault.

This work was carried out by a team of volunteers and it did not take long before we penetrated the roof of a vault at a depth of about three feet. We had the use of an endoscope and special lighting equipment, kindly loaned by the Royal Air Force. With the aid of these, plus the specialist knowledge of an engineer, we were able to confirm the vault to measure approximately 12ft. long by 8ft. wide and 8ft. high. Access was gained via 13 steps leading from an entrance at the west end of the Bernard memorial slab.

Our observations led us to believe there were about a dozen coffins of the 18th century period. This seemed to confirm what Halliwell-Phillipps had said - that the vault had been taken over by the Thursbys. Naturally, we assumed the first of the Thursby family to be buried in the vault would be the judge - the man who had bought the manor from John Bernard and died in 1700. It could have been at this particular time that the decision was taken to remove the coffins of John Bernard, his two wives and those of his children.

You can imagine how we all felt. Were the remains of Shakespeare's granddaughter to be found in the vault below?

Now came the waiting period. The necessary faculty had been applied for to permit us to enter the vault, but such things take time. This gave me opportunity to ponder over the question of where to look next should our investigation of the vault prove fruitless. The only other clue to the possible whereabouts of the Bernards was the chancel. John Bernard's mother married twice and, after the death of her first husband, Baldwin, in 1660, she married Sir Edmund Hampton. In the chancel there is a monumental plaque on the north wall which states: "Buried near this spot and underneath are the remains of Baldwin Bernards".

The Bernards had taken over the whole of the east end of the church for the burial of their dead. The result was that there was the vault at the east end of the south aisle, another beneath the sanctuary and a third under what is now the Lady Chapel in the north aisle. The latter used to be the Chantry Chapel and this, in all probability, was the first of the Bernard family vaults.

The Chantry Chapel was extended some 10 feet eastward during the late 16th century and the work may have been carried out to enable the existing vault to be extended in the same direction. This alteration would still allow the vault to be beneath the extended Chantry Chapel where the priest would sing mass for the souls of those who had held the endowment. At one time, these vaults would have been more visible than they are today. In the 19th century the church was partially destroyed by a great storm. Almost 70 per cent of it had to be rebuilt and the floor re-laid. As a result of the storm damage and the re-building work which followed, certain memorial tablets may have been damaged beyond repair. Others that survived would have been put back on the walls, but whether they were fitted into their original positions is questionable.

To my way of thinking, any re-interment of the remains of Sir John and his two wives and children would have been carried out by William Thursby, the judge. If there had to be any removal, the judge, as a man of law, would have seen to it that everything was conducted in a legal manner. That would require paper work and he would have had to inform the rector of his intention, even though he was Lord of the Manor. But no such information has come to light, so we had to rely on our own investigations.

All this speculation was put aside when the faculty came through. Friday, February 13, 1981, was the day earmarked for the opening.

The vault's covering slab, which was four inches thick, was lifted from its position beneath the second pew from the front in the south aisle. With this safely propped up, two electric examination lamps were switched on and taken down the steps into the vault by my research assistant, Mrs. Joan Neal, the first person to officially enter it for 140 years.

Then myself and the other members of the team went down the steps. We were all surprised how dry the vault was, helped by the two air vents, one in the east wall and the other in the south wall. The measurements were more or less as previously stated and the place was complete with an arched roof. There, in front of us, were nine lead-lined coffins - all still sealed, with the exception of one.

To the left of the steps, and against the north wall, were two children's coffins, one extremely small and possibly that of a child who died shortly after birth. On the opposite side, against the south wall, was a third child's coffin. The nine adult coffins were in two tiers of four, while a third tier had only one, which like those on the second, rested on iron bars set into two partitioning walls.

All but one had an inscription plate, while another had only the year "1733" visible. Of the children's coffins, only the one on the south side could be identified - a four-month old child of the Thursby family, as shown by the family crest on the lid. The odd thing was that there was no coffin containing William Thursby, the judge who died February 4,1700, aged 72, and whose monumental memorial stands above the vault.

The pathologists offered their opinions about the person's remains in the coffin with no nameplate - it was a boy in his early teens. This view was reached after they had examined a portion of skull and pieces of bone. According to Mr. John Langley, writing in the parish magazine of June, 1981, these could have been the remains of Benjamin Thursby, one of the sons of John Harvey Thursby the first. Benjamin was buried at Abington on September 2,1760. He was 16. The three children's coffins, he suggested, were of the offsprings of the same John Harvey Thursby and his wife, Honor, who lost four of their 12 children as babies.

The adult coffins were those of Audrey Thursby, died July 12, 1704, aged 67, the second wife of William Thursby; John Harvey Thursby, died September 12,1798, aged 65; Sophia Francis Thursby, died May 22,1827, aged 20; Master Henry Thursby, died May 6,1782, aged 11 years; Colonel William Thursby, died September 15,1827, aged 58. The only one on the third tier was that of Annie Armytage, who died October 28,1840, aged 73, daughter of John Harvey Thursby the second and his wife, Anne.

It was suggested by Mr. Langley that the 1733 coffin was that of Jane Thursby, wife of John, a half brother of William, for she was buried on September 6,1733. After all that, there was still no trace of any Bernards. Where could they be? That was the question now confronting us.

We moved to the chancel, making borings for the endoscope and light. The only vault to be found, of any significant, was beneath the sanctuary and immediately below the alter. In it could be seen only one coffin, with a sword resting on top. This, I suspect, is the resting place of Sir Robert Bernard, a cousin of Sir John's, Knight and Baronet and Serjeant at Law, who was given a state funeral. He died in 1666 "upon the 18 day of April at his loggings at Serjeants Inn in Fleet Street, London."

Beneath the chancel is a brick-lined grave, which is probably that of the Rev. Charles Thursby, who was buried at Abington on May 20,1783. Below the choir stalls is the burial place of Henry Lowth, gent., who was appointed steward of all the estates of William Thursby in the latter's last will and testament. Henry Lowth died November 17, 1737, aged 86.

Once again our investigations proved to be fruitless, so we turned our efforts to the only place left - the Lady Chapel. Here are to be seen two table tombs to Sir John Bernard's mother and her second husband, Sir John Hampden. The tombs stand along the south wall of the chapel, having been moved there from their orginal place in the centre many years ago. Here on the north wall, between two windows, is a memorial to Richard Thursby, a son of Downhall Thursby, who died on May 24,1736, aged 68. On the same wall, but further to the west, is a tablet to J.H. Thursby, who died June 1,1764, and to his wife, Honor Harvey Thursby, daughter of Robert Pigott Esq., of Chetwyn, Salop. She died on September 24,1781, aged 68.

The tablet states they are buried "under this monument".

In the meantime, we were waiting a second faculty permitting us to open the vault beneath the Lady Chapel, which we had found by means of the endoscope and light, and also the steps leading into it. This proved to be a long way off, but it eventually came, and, on the evening of June 28, 1981, work was started on opening the entrance by civil engineer,

John Thompson. It proved to be far more difficult than expected. Four small slabs had to be lifted, and, beneath these, was a four-inch layer of grit filling. Even when this was removed, the work was not over, for we then came across yet another slab. Gaining entrance to this vault was not proving as easy as the one in the south aisle. Eventually, we got the last slab up, revealing a hole of about 18 ins. x 18 ins. and a drop of about four feet to the first step.

By now it was late at night and we made the opening safe for the full team to be there for the investigations the following morning. What would we find? Would the mystery of the missing Bernards be solved, or could it be yet another disappointment? We spent a restless night waiting impatiently for the morrow.

The following morning we arrived at the church early. The small opening was quite a squeeze and, when we got down, taking the inspection lamps with us, we found ourselves in a smaller vault than the Thursby one in the south aisle. Also, while the other vault floor was slabbed, this one just consisted of earth. Its height was a mere 5ft 10ins, at the apex, and, with so little room to move, only two people at a time could work there. There were seven adult coffins and four of children. All but one adult coffin was open caused chiefly by corrosion of the lead lining. The outer woodwork fell to dust at a touch.

Ventilation was not as good as in the Thursby vault and we had to keep going up through the opening for air. On the extreme right were two coffins, one resting on the other and the top one bore the nameplate "John Harvey Thursby, Obit June 1,1764, aged 54 years." This was the only coffin intact.

The bottom coffin contained the bones of a woman, said the pathologist after an examination of the bones seen through the opened side. It seems likely that these were the remains of Thursby's wife, Honor, but it was not possible to move the top coffin to inspect the nameplate on the lid. Next in line on the floor was a coffin of a male, and next to that one of a female, said the pathologist. While no nameplate could be found on either, parts of the disintegrated armorial crest could be identified as that of the Hampdens. It can be stated with reasonable certainty, then, that, the coffins contained the remains of Sir Edmund Hampden Knight, who died December 21,1627, and his wife, Dame Elinor Hampden, who departed this life on June 27,1634.

Dame Elinor, in fact, was previously the wife of Sir Bernard's father, Baldwin, and the mother of Sir John. She also became the mother of three sons by her second marriage, as well as bearing Baldwin two sons and a daughter, John, William and Catherine.

After the Hampden coffins, we came to what proved to be the most interesting part of our investigations at Abington Church. Next to Dame Elinor was another coffin, with a sixth alongside and a seventh on top. The sixth coffin had collapsed under the weight of the seventh which had sunk into it. Stacked on top of these were three children's coffins, while a fourth had fallen down the back of those containing the adults. It looked as if the fifth, sixth and seventh coffins, and those of the four infants, had been dumped there from another site.

Some confirmation of this can be drawn from the "line-up" of the first four coffins - the Thursbys and Hampdens. Of the Thursbys, John Harvey died first (1764), yet his coffin rests on that of his wife who died in 1781. According to the dates, he should have been the first to be placed there, and his wife alongside 17 years later. The Hampdens are in correct datal order. Could it be, then, that the Hampdens were (upto a date unknown) the only occupants of the vault, and that the two Thursbys were brought in from another resting place? Undoubtedly, the north side of the Hampdens was earmarked for "infilling" by the other coffins found there.

These last three adult coffins produced the answer to the riddle of the missing Bernards. Next to Dame Elinor lay the missing Sir John Barnard, according to our findings, for the pathologist identified the bones of those of a male of about 70 years. Part of the Bernard family crest still showed on the corroding coffin. The coffin next to Sir John's was the one which our investigations indicated contained the remains of Shakespeare's missing granddaughter, Lady Elizabeth. The bones were those of a woman in her 60s who apparently suffered from an arthritic complaint, said the pathologist.

The remains in the seventh coffin were clearly those of Sir John's first wife who died in 1642. They were identified as those of a woman in her early 30s. The evidence showed that the latter three coffins had, at a previous time, been elsewhere. Without doubt, they were in the south aisle vault that was once one of the resting places of the long line of the Bernards of Abington, and were removed to make way for the Thursbys.

The clues are in the dates of death - Sir John 1674, Shakespeare's granddaughter 1670 and Elizabeth Bernard (the first) 1642. In their first resting place they would have been in the correct order (1642,1670,1674), but when they were taken out for the sake of convenience, they would have been transferred in reverse order. The coffins of the four children were almost certainly those of the offspring of Sir John's first wife, although only one of them still bore the Bernard crest.

Why were John Harvey Thursby and his wife, Honor, laid in the vault beneath the Lady Chapel? This I cannot answer. Another question the reader may ask is: Where is Baldwin Bernard and his first wife? My guess is that they were not far away from where we were in the Lady Chapel vault. I think that, if we could have made a hole in the vault's east wall, we would have come across another vault. There, I feel sure, we would have found Baldwin and his wife - and possibly others of the Bernard line.

In my view, the north aisle vault was much bigger than the other in which we stood and, certainly, the east wall gave signs of being hastily built. However, the investigation was over. At long last, the whereabouts of the Bernards - and, in particular, Shakespeare's granddaughter - had, to my mind, been established.

It had taken several months of strenuous teamwork to achieve this end, but everyone concerned was happy at a job well done. We finally closed the vault to leave the remains of those beneath to lie in peace. Today, in the Church of St. Peter and Paul, Abington, a plaque marks the spot where our discovery was made. Despite finding the remains of Shakespeare's granddaughter, we were disappointed at not uncovering anything tangible about Elizabeth's grandfather. I began to wonder if something may have been overlooked.

It had been said that Lady Bernard was seen leaving her grandfather's home with papers and books "for safe keeping in Northamptonshire," soon after his death. "For safe keeping in Northamptonshire" could mean only one thing - she was taking them back to Abington Manor. Such items were kept in secret places known only to the people concerned, so there must have been such a hiding place at Abington. The question was, where?

Others had thought of this in the past, but their efforts to locate such a hiding place had proved fruitless. We thought there was the possibility of a secret passage between the house and the nearby church, standing only a matter of yards away. With this in mind, I asked Mr. William Terry, curator of the Northampton Museums and Art Gallery, for permission to make a search. He willingly gave his consent, and, to our surprise, revealed that over the years, there had been rumours of a passage, but no-one had ever found it.

It was a sunny winter's day when we made the 20-mile journey to Abington Manor, now a museum, to explore the area and the old house, the east side of the building having been re-built by the Thursby family in about 1690. A morning's investigation enabled us to map out a line where we believed the passage might be and than go into the cellar to locate the point where it started. This proved to be the oldest part of the cellar.

Permission was given for us to return with other members of the team to start exploratory drilling. On the following Saturday, we started drilling the cellar wall, hoping for success. But the first hole brought no result. We were going through really thick ironstone. Another spot, six inches lower than the first was chosen, and, within a short while, we were delighted to see the drill extension slide through the hole with ease - a sure indication that there was a space behind the wall.

A second hole was made nearby in what we realised was brickwork. Part of this broke away, enabling us to shine a torch through and to see what was beyond. It was a tunnel. Not as high as the one at Rushton Hall, but apparently well constructed and arched. However, we could not see very far, only about 10 feet and the tunnel then took what appeared to be a left-hand bend.

The floor seemed to be composed of earth and there was a mound of rubble immediately behind the opening we had made, probably the remains from when that end of the tunnel was bricked up. According to the type of brick used, this was around the end of the 17th century. From a cursory inspection by the light of the torch, the tunnel was very old. We estimated it must have been built about 1550, when the Bernards were Lords of the Manor of Abington.

We were amazed at the amount of fresh air coming out of the aperture we had made and we dearly wanted to make the opening wider so that we could go in, but we needed permission first. Mr. Terry, the curator, was just as excited as we were over the discovery and gave his consent to widen the entrance, although we had to wait until the following weekend.

When the next Saturday came around, everyone arrived on time, eager to widen the hole in the cellar wall and inspect the tunnel. Immediately the opening had been enlarged, three of the team, Tony Woodford, Steve Barney and Michael Bindley, wearing suitable headgear and each armed with a torch and trailing an inspection lamp, crawled in.

The tunnel measured 3 ft 10 ins in height, with the arch starting at the 3 ft mark, while the width was 3 ft 7 ins. The walling was of the dry-walling type, but with a mortar fixer at the back, while the arch was lime-mortared. It was from the latter that what appeared to be stalactites had formed to a depth of about three inches. Some time later the three-man team returned and reported on the state of the tunnel which they said appeared to be in first-class condition. Further along its length they noticed that they had more headroom, while at half-way there was a shaft in the roof with a "T" junction which was assumed to be an air vent. This could have accounted for the fresh air blowing along the tunnel.

The most amazing discovery, however, came when they crawled out into a round chamber, also dry-walled, where they could stand up with ease. They said they thought the height of the chamber was about 7 ft with a diameter of 6 ft.

Later, it was found that about 18 inches below the earth floor of the chamber was the actual ironstone flooring, thus providing a full height of about 8 ft 6 ins.

The roof comprised two stone slabs, and there was a long iron bar which had been pushed through the crack of the slabs. Going into the grounds, the bar was seen sticking out of the centre of the lawn between the museum and the main road. The team had also taken a long coil of rope with them for safety reasons and they used this to measure the length of the tunnel, which was a surprising 107ft. It must have been used as an escape route, for the entrance was via the hearth of the fireplace which once stood in the room immediately above the opening we had made in the cellar wall.

Just above the opening could be seen two cavities - one on either side. Across the top of one was a stone slab, indicating part of the original hearth. This was almost certainly the means of egress to the tunnel, while the one on the other side possibly led into the original chimney. It is thought that the chamber at the end of the tunnel was once beneath an ornate garden-piece through which the escapee could make his exit after crawling along the tunnel. There was no sign of a ladder or any other means of climbing out of the chamber.

Various pieces of glass were found, including the neck of an old phial, its irridescence indicating it had lain there, according to a glass expert, for 200 to 300 years. Also, in the rubble behind the wall where we had made the opening, we discovered the base of a very thick wine bottle, which was dated late 17th century - about the time the tunnel opening was bricked up. The discovery of the tunnel was exciting, but it was a pity no papers or books were found.

Could it be that there is another tunnel or hide waiting to be discovered, containing relics associated with Shakespeare which his granddaughter had taken from her grandfather's home "for sake-keeping in Northamptonshire?". Only time will tell.

After considerable thought, I came to the conclusion that, originally, the tunnel was built as an outlet for some other purpose, probably a sewer. In that case, the other chamber at the other end would be the collecting point for the refuse which had solidified over the centuries.

However, the cavity beneath the fireplace, suggests the passageway was also used as an escape route. As to its age, after examination by experts, our guess of circa 1550 was found to be way out. According to the men of knowledge, it was no later than the Saxon era, which makes it all the more interesting.

What sort of building stood on this site at that period of history? That is a question which will probably never be answered.

CHAPTER 7

A lost diary

There is one particular record, if it could be found, which might throw light on the life of Shakespeare. This is the missing Throckmorton Diary.

Sir Arthur Throckmorton, who lived at Paulersperry, Northampton, was a great diarist, and two of his diaries were discovered in Canterbury, where his eldest daughter lived, some years ago. One of these covered the period from 1578 to 1595 and the other from 1609 to 1613 - 13 years before his death. It is the one from 1595 to 1609 which would reveal particularly interesting notes about life in England during that period and possibly something about the private and public life of the playwright himself.

These years are important for they take in the Essex conspiracy and, of course, the Gunpowder Plot. Therefore, it was natural to turn our attention to the village church of Paulersperry where Sir Arthur is buried. His vault is to be found beneath the chapel on the north side of the chancel and, on visiting the church, we were soon able to locate its exact position.

We explained our work to the rector and made a request through him to the parochial church council for permission to carry out preliminary investigations and, if agreeable, eventually to bore the necessary holes and use an optical fibre rod to investigate the contents. This rod carries a small but extremely powerful light. It allows the user not only to have a look around the vault, but also to take photographs and video film of the interior.

But the church council refused permission, the first time

that such a refusal had been given. I even offered to go to talk to the church council to explain personally our work, but to no avail. If Sir Arthur did take the missing diary with him to the grave, then it still lies there, its covers firmly closed.

Where else could the missing diary be? If Sir Arthur's eldest daughter had two of them, it was possible that another daughter received the other. Looking up the records of the Throckmorton family, I found that Sir Arthur's second daughter, Ann, had married Sir Peter Temple, of Stowe, Buckinghamshire. Could it be that she had the other diary?

I contacted the rector, the Rev. Michael Drury, who, along with his parochial church council, agreed to an investigation. Eventually, we found the location of the temple vault below the chapel on the north side of the chancel. Here was a raised wooden floor and, finding a loose board at the eastern end of where we felt the vault was, we began drilling. After a while, we realised that the drill was continuously going through brick and that we were possibly going down the outer wall of the vault. So, we moved the drill to a spot a few inches westward and struck lucky, going through the vault roof very quickly. Needless to say, we were excited at such an early discovery and we made a second hole nearby. Inserting a thin rod with a light bulb down one hole and an endoscope down the other, we had a limited view of the inside of the vault.

This did not help a great deal, so I contacted the firm with the optical fibre rod. They came to our aid and, with their more sophisticated equipment, which included a close circuit TV, we were able to see on the screen what lay below our feet. The vault was extremely well built and contained a number of coffins. They were not in rows; some were on top of each other and others were laid singly on the floor.

But there was one which mystified everyone. The vault contained an alcove - something we had not seen in any other vault - and in it there was a coffin, standing vertical. I cannot offer an explanation. The entrance steps could be seen clearly and it was estimated that the point of access was immediately below the apex of the arch near the chancel arch.

The following week we returned to the church to try to locate the entrance slab to the vault. Needless to say, everyone was excited at the prospects of what lay ahead and were ready for the work in hand. First, the floorboards were carefully taken up and numbered for replacing. Then the earth and rubble were removed. This was not difficult, with everyone setting to it with a will. But there was no covering slab. Instead, we discovered the entrance tunnel leading to the steps had been filled in with large pieces of stone, some of which appeared to have come from the old part of the church. There were pieces of brick and rubble, all of which appeared to have been cemented, while earth had been thrown in as fill-in.

It seemed the work had been done with one object in mind - to ensure no future access would be gained at this entrance point. Just the same, we decided to have a go at removing the blocked passage. For three hours, we laboured in turns, chiselling away the cement, removing the earth, stones and brick pieces, but it proved to be an exceptionally slow job with little impression to show for our labours.

Our civil engineer, Mr John Thompson, estimated it would take two full days of work to remove at least half a ton of in-filling. Reluctantly, it was agreed that it would do no good to carry on, and that the work should be abandoned - at least, for now. Everything taken out of the entrance was replaced. The ground was levelled and covered over as we had found it and the floorboards put back.

Some days later, Mr Thompson sent a report to the parochial church council explaining in detail how an easier access could be made into the vault. But it would have cost too much. As a voluntary team, with no funds to back us, except out of our own pockets, it was felt we could not meet such an expense. For the time being, at any rate, Stowe Parish Church had to be put behind us.

It was a big disappointment, particularly in view of all the hard work which had been put in.

On the video film, there appeared to be an object between two of the coffins. It looked like a small box. Also, we wanted to check the number of coffins, because what we had seen on the video did not tally with the list of the names of those buried inside.

Another interesting point was the fact that the vault was not started until October 6,1672. Anne Temple, Sir Arthur

Throckmorton's daughter, died in childbirth on January 20, 1619 - 52 years before the vault was built - and she is listed as having been placed in the vault. In fact, her name and date of death heads the list of 14 interred.

Therefore, for more than half a century, she must have rested elsewhere. Likewise, her husband, Sir Peter Temple, who died in 1653, and two others, must have been buried somewhere else before being moved. Perhaps the vault is just an extension of an older one? Or, perhaps, it is the original vault and it has an extension? The answers may not be known in the foreseeable future, unless the opportunity arises for work to be resumed. And, the mystery of the upright coffin, held in place in its alcove by iron bars, remains unsolved.

Confusion reigned when we began investigations into Lady Elizabeth Carey, of Church Stowe, Stowe Nine Churches in Northamptonshire. During preliminary work, we were under the impression that Lady Elizabeth, whose vault was said to be beneath the Chancel of St. Michael's Church in this lovely village, was the same person who had been closely associated with the poets of her time.

The Lady Elizabeth Carey in whom we were interested, was second daughter of Sir John Spencer, of Althorp. Included among her close friends was Edmund Spenser (1553-1599), who was one of the foremost poets of those days and became particularly famous for his "Faerie Queen" which he finished at his home in Kilcolman, Co. Cork.

Despite the different spelling of Spenser and Spencer, the poet was a kinsman of Lady Elizabeth Carey, and it is probable that they both knew Shakespeare. Spenser was the elder son of Lord John Spenser and he died in poverty after returning from Ireland. The Earl of Essex paid for his funeral and he lies near Chaucer in Westminster Abbey.

Lady Elizabeth corrected much of Spenser's works, as well as those of Thomas Hash (1567-1601), who was really a satirist, and could be called the father of the English novel. Her husband was George Carey, the eldest son of Henry Carey, the first Lord Hunsden. She died about 1618 and is also buried in Westminster Abbey, somewhere near Poets

Corner. This news dashed any hope we might have had of investigating her burial place.

It was while we were carrying out our enquiries into Lady Elizabeth Carey that we came across the surprising revelation that there were two Lady Elizabeth Careys, both living within a short distance of each other. The second Lady Elizabeth married Edmund Carey, of Moulton Park, Northamptonshire, the brother of George Carey.

Sir Edmund Carey and his Lady Elizabeth lived at the Manor at Church Stowe, but, although there is an exceptionally fine monument to her in St. Michael's Church, there is no indication of where her husband was buried. There is no mention of him in the Dictionary of National Biography.

The Lady Elizabeth of Church Stowe was, to say the least, a remarkable woman. She lived right through the Elizabethan period and way into the Stuart monarchy, dying in 1630 at the age of 84. Her monumental tomb in St. Michael's Church is said to be among the finest in the country and was commissioned by Lady Elizabeth herself nine years before her death. It shows her in a reclining position and was the work of the eminent English sculptor, Nicholas Stone, who was to become master-mason to Charles 1.

Before marrying Edmund Carey, Lady Elizabeth was the wife of Sir John Danvers, of Dauntsey, Wiltshire, by whom she had three sons, Charles, Henry and John. Charles was born in 1568 and, as well as being a soldier, he was also an actor. For a time, he was with the Chamberlain's Company, of which William Shakespeare was a member. It can be assumed, therefore, that Charles knew him, along with such others as Nash and Spenser.

From this, it can be seen that, when she eventually married Edmund Carey and become sister-in-law to the other Lady Elizabeth Carey (George's wife), there must have been a close affinity between the women because of their respective connections with playwrights and poets. Like his brother, Sir Charles, Henry led an active and interesting life. He was born at Dauntsey on June 28, 1573, and, while still a youth, was a page to Sir Philip Sidney. Later, he served under the man later to become Prince of Orange. At the Siege of

Rouen (1591), Henry was knighted for his services in the field, at the tender age of 18.

Charles and Henry became involved in a dispute in Wiltshire in which a certain Henry Long was killed. It would seem that Long was dining with friends in a house at Corsham when the two brothers and a number of retainers burst into the room and Long was shot dead. The brothers fled on horseback to Whitley Lodge, near Titchfield, home of Henry Wriothesley, third Earl of Southampton, a personal friend. Southampton was also a proven patron of Shakespeare - so we are back again to the bard.

Through the efforts of the earl, the brothers succeeded, after some days, in making their way out of the country. A unique quote reads: "Henceforth Charles was exceedingly devoted to the Earl of Southampton upon affection first begun upon the deserving of the same earl towards him when he was in trouble about the murder of one Long."

Henry and Charles went to France, where King Henry IV received them and interceded with Queen Elizabeth on their behalf. He also wrote to Sir Robert Cecil to try to get the Order of Banishment, which had been against them, reversed. Eventually, that is what happened and they returned to England in 1598. Henry served in Ireland soon after and became Governor of Armagh in 1601. He was created Baron Danvers of Dauntsey by James 1 for his valiant services in Ireland. He went on to hold a number of other important posts and, in February 1626, was created Earl of Denby by Charles 1.

Charles, following his return to England, became involved with Essex in a rebellion against Elizabeth and, for this, both were executed. This must have caused considerable grief to Lady Elizabeth Carey - a remarkable woman, as already stated, who had known many notable and influential people during her long life.

I decided to try to find the place in St. Michael's Church where she had been buried and preliminary investigations began near her monumental tomb in October, 1982. This proved fruitless, despite drilling to a depth of six feet, so we moved our attention to the north chapel, where the result was again negative. Here we struck extremely hard material which the drill was unable to penetrate. That left the south chapel, and we concentrated our efforts on this from the disused stoke room. We went through two layers of brickwork when, suddenly, the drill found a cavity and then hit another obstacle - a wall.

Permission was obtained to knock out some of the bricks of the first wall, only to discover that the cavity reached to the floor of the church and came out in the south aisle via one of the gratings of the old heating system. The second wall was also of brick and, although we drilled to a length of five feet six inches, we failed to hit any further space.

On our next drilling, we moved about 12 inches to the left, going through three layers of brick before striking ironstone. A further 12 inches through this and we went into space - a vault. The brickwork and ironstone were then chiselled out, a lengthy and arduous job because of the confined working space. Eventually, a hole was made wide enough for our photographer, Steve Barney, to put his camera through, aided by a rod light. Then, helped by a mirror on a long pole, a rough survey was made of the interior.

The roof appeared to be barrel-shaped and patched in places with lime mortar. In the far left-hand corner, and practically beneath Lady Elizabeth Carey's monument, was a lead-lined coffin. Another one, or what remained of it, lay on the right-hand side. There were a number of bones and skulls lying around the floor. They may have come from another vault, or they may have been uncovered when the ground was dug out to make way for the steps leading down to the stoke room. This discovery was made on November 13,1982, but it was not until February 18,1983, after official permission had been given, that the hole was opened sufficiently wide enough to crawl through.

Before carrying out any investigations, all the loose bones were gathered up, put in plastic sacks, and placed neatly in the vault. The wood casing of the two coffins had rotted and fallen off. This was put in sacks and left there. Then we were able to turn our attention to the two coffins themselves. Here we found the lead to be surprisingly thick in comparison to others seen in other places, but it had split open.

On examining the bones in the coffin on the right-hand

side, the pathologists agreed they were of a woman, probably between 30 and 40 years of age. Her reddish brown hair was still intact and plaited. To the surprise of everyone, the pathologists said some of the bones were not those of a human being, but possibly a dog! Perhaps the lady's pet had died at the same time and had been placed with her in the coffin.

Going over to the other coffin, in which the arms had been laid straight down the sides of the body instead of crossed over, the pathologists agreed the bones were also of a woman. The age at death was estimated as late 70s or early 80s. There were no signs of arthritis and the indications were that the woman had been healthy for her age. From this diagnosis, it was the view that they were the remains of Lady Elizabeth Carey, whose hair was wound in a bun on the skull, with no sign of any pins to hold it in place. Some small pieces of material were found in the coffin, but these fell to shreds at a touch.

It had been hoped that the other coffin might have been that of Sir Charles Danvers and that a Shakespearean artefact might have been found, but there was nothing at all of such a nature. But the question remains, who is the mystery woman on the right? Could she have been a relative of Lady Elizabeth's or of Edmund Carey? Certainly, she must have been close to the family.

After our work in the vault had been completed, it was the re-sealed.

While awaiting permission to enter the vault, we were not idle. Beneath the chapel we came across what we believe to be a Norman crypt (the present church is built on the site of a church of a considerably older building) stretching down the centre of the chancel from the east window for 12 feet or more, and with an entrance between the choir stalls.

We were able to survey the interior by means of a borescope which Key Med (Medical and Industrial Equipment) Ltd., of Southend-an-Sea, loaned especially for the task. Both the east and west end walls of the crypt were of rough stone facing and the opinion was that the west end was the outer wall of the Saxon church and, when extended by the Normans, a crypt was built beneath the chancel. At a much later date, it was used as a vault, for four coffins were to be seen.

So, although no Shakespearean find was made at St. Michael's, at least the months of hard work had resulted in some success.

CHAPTER 8

A house near the river

Henley Street, with its three-gabled cottage, is the shrine of pilgrims to Stratford seeking Shakespeare's birthplace.

Yet, over the years, there have been arguments, many of them heated, about this house and its right to such a claim. In 1913, Henry Shelley published his book, Shakespeare & Stratford, and raised doubts: "There is an older tradition which is fatal to the claims of the Henley Street house", he wrote. "A late echo of that tradition sounded in the ears of Washington Irving, for did not the old sexton express 'a doubt' as to the genuineness of the birthplace?"

Shelley recalls the "lore of the learned and industrious William Oldys" who, in the first quarter of the 18th century, had recorded a tradition to the effect that Shakespeare was born in a house near the churchyard, and this legend persisted until the 19th century. Shelley continues: "A house near the river, as the laborious J.C. Halliwell-Phillips wrote, called the Brook House, now pulled down, was some years since asserted to have been the birthplace of Shakespeare." He adds: "What makes matters still worse for the Henley Street shrine is that the earliest visitors who were drawn to Stratford-on-Avon by the fame of Shakespeare entirely ignored its existence."

Let me say here and now that I do not subscribe to the belief that Brook House was the birthplace of the poet. The only thing I would say about the story is that Brook House obviously existed and, from conversions with the archivist at Stratford-on-Avon Records Office, in addition to examination of manuscripts from the mid-18th century, it appears that Brook House stood in the vicinity of Southern Lane and Waterside, almost opposite the Royal Shakespeare Theatre. In July, 1768, the deeds mention the house by the river, but it is not until more than 100 years later, in 1898, that we have a schedule of documents relating to a garden in Chapel Lane, listing the number of the house. This ground is now known as the summerhouse garden next to the Arden Hotel in Chapel Lane.

With this information and the permission of the Shakespeare Memorial Theatre, I suggested an archaeological survey on the garden to try to find the foundations of Brook House. I obtained the help of the RAF Reconnaissance Unit at Huntingdon who took photographs at 2,000 ft showing what appeared to be a straight line in the garden (a part of the foundations?) and, to the right of the line, what looked very much like an old bomb crater; in my opinion, this was the cellar of the house. The survey began just before Christmas, 1985. Little was I to realise that it would be more than two years before our work was completed.

The garden measured 133 ft in length and 80 ft wide and was virtually all turf. We tried to decide the approximate position of the house, but the old maps I had were no help; all they showed were a number of houses which stood along the waterside in front of the garden.

However, on our second visit, we decided to dig pilot holes the length of the garden in the hope that we would find some clues. As luck would have it, the third borehole showed that, behind the main retaining wall - which is at street level - there was a second wall. Bricks could be dated with reasonable accuracy to the late 16th century, but the puzzle was that the 16th century bricks went down only halfway. After this, there was Gloucestershire stone and, to the right of where we were digging, was a stone lintel, suggesting a window or doorway. I thought we had found the front wall of a house, but I could not prove beyond reasonable doubt that it was Brook House.

The cellar was particularly interesting to me. Although it appeared on the RAF photographs (and on some infra-red photos taken later) that it had been filled with broken brick, there was still a chance we would find an artefact to help us understand William Shakespeare and his family better.

I wonder why John Shakespeare left the house by the river. Perhaps it was too noisy - and too smelly! The Avon was wider at that point and there was sewage flowing down Chapel Lane into the river. Boats were being loaded and unloaded and there was a lot of activity and mosquitoes. Even in England, malaria could be contracted from the female mosquito in those days. Perhaps it all became too much for John and his wife, Mary, and they decided to move to a more sensible and sociable place - the house in Henley Street where William was born.

In November, 1986, the second stage of the investigation into the site of the Brook House began. The wall we had found earlier proved to be early 19th century, built on top of the remains of the front of a house and used as a garden wall. The bricks were made locally and the difference in age of manufacture could be plainly seen.

It is recorded that Brook House was "pulled down" in 1769, the same year as David Garrick's jubilee, but our subsequent investigations offered a more dramatic reason for its demise.

A drawing by John Jordan (1746-1809) showed what remained of Brook House after a fire destroyed it. This drawing also showed a gazebo, a summer house and a wall incorporating the remains of two bay windows of Brook House. We decided to excavate for evidence of a fire; this would be powerful support to our theory that we were standing on the site of Brook House. And, as we dug down and got within three feet of floor level, we found large deposits of soot and pitch melted over stone, alongwith charred pieces of timber.

On further investigation, we discovered the remains of a small cobblestone courtyard at the rear of the site and parts of a cobbled pathway, leading to Waterside. The depth of these varied from 2 ft to 7 ft.

The discovery of the charred timbers and soot convinced me that we had, indeed, come across the foundations of Brook House; it tied in with Jordan's notes about the fire which destroyed the building and I am pleased to say that the evidence was sufficiently convincing for the Mayor of Stratford to unveil a plaque on April 23, 1988 at the Arden Hotel. The plaque marked the site of Brook House, unknown for 200 years.

It is interesting to add that this is where it is believed Shakespeare wrote the scene of the ghost in Hamlet, so finding it was a significant contribution to the quest for knowledge about the poet.

The Brook House discovery, the location of Susanna Hall's tomb, the finding of another Mr W.H. and the discovery of the coffin bearing Mary Fitton's pansy crest are all clues to answering the questions about the life and times of William Shakespeare. We have a clear picture of his relationship with the Dark Lady of the sonnets and the youthful Mr W.H. It was tempestuous, as his own fair hand relates. The fact that another William Herbert, close to Shakespeare, with the plain title of "Mr", was alive at the time of the sonnets is particularly relevant. For centuries, scholars never suspected this. The Earl of Pembroke was chosen as the Fair Youth because his name was William Herbert and he matched the initials, although his title did not fit. Now, at last, perhaps history can be re-written.

William Herbert associates Mary Fitton with Shakespeare.

Herbert married into the Fitton family and was probably introduced to Shakespeare by Mary, who was such a prominent figure at court. Mary would have presented herself frequently on the London scene. As a maid of honour, she would have visited the theatres to see the plays of Shakespeare and she would have been in his company during the day at court. They cannot have failed to meet and, such was the allure of Mary, that he would have been a cold fish, indeed, if her charms had not lit a flame in his heart.

Consider the deep emotion in his plays and sonnets. It is not necessary to explain in terms used by a psychologist (as some have tried in the past) the state of Shakespeare's mind. Simply acredit his great works to the driving force and inspiration given to him by this woman. She is responsible for this emptiness and excitement. Reading his plays, I feel the despair he suffered when the Dark Lady chose to play fast and loose with his affections. He believed all she told him, but this was his undoing. She did not care for one man in particular; she loved many. All this woman wanted was power and money.

And yet, there was a period in her life when it seems she did love Shakespeare. I am counting on that brief, passionate encounter to provide the evidence that Mary Fitton and the Dark Lady were one. The answer may lie in that tomb at Gawsworth.

EPILOGUE

The grave-digger at Gawsworth saw the young woman enter the church as he sank his spade into the ground. He carried on digging for a while and then, as the heat of the June afternoon raised beads of perspiration on his ageing brow, he broke off to watch a skylark wheeling up above.

He turned towards the church and, through the partly opened door, he noticed the woman kneeling, as if in prayer. She wore a green velvet riding habit and a large green hat with a white plume.

The grave-digger returned to his spade. The air was still and, but for the skylark, all was quiet.

An hour passed and it was time to head for home. But first, the church door must be locked. The woman still knelt in her pew but turned to look at the old man as he reached the entrance. "Come along, Miss, I have to close the church", he said. She seemed to hear him but not a word came from her pale lips.

The grave-digger was struck by the extreme sadness in her eyes and asked: "Is anything the matter, Miss?" There was no reply; only the dull ring of the church clock striking the hour as the woman faded away before his eyes ....

(Villagers at Gawsworth tell of a ghostly figure in a riding habit who is occasionally seen moving from the direction of the rectory to the nearby church. Mary Fitton's bedroom was in the rectory. Is her grave in the church?)